PENTECOST 2

**INTERPRETING
THE LESSONS OF
THE CHURCH YEAR**

**JOHN H. P.
REUMANN**

**PROCLAMATION 5
SERIES B**

PROCLAMATION

FORTRESS PRESS   MINNEAPOLIS

PROCLAMATION 5
Interpreting the Lessons of the Church Year
Series B, Pentecost 2

Scripture quotations, unless translated from the Greek by the author, are from the New Revised Standard Version Bible, copyright © 1989 by the Division of Christian Education of the National Council of the Churches of Christ in the U.S.A. and used by permission.

Cover and interior design: Spangler Design Team

Library of Congress Cataloging-in-Publication Data available

ISBN 0-8006-4191-4

The paper used in this publication meets the minimum requirements of American National Standard for Information Sciences—Permanence of Paper for Printed Library Materials, ANSI Z329.48-1984.   (∞)™

Manufactured in the U.S.A.   AF 1-4191

98   97   96   95   94   1   2   3   4   5   6   7   8   9   10

CONTENTS

OVERVIEW OF LECTIONARY READINGS

PENTECOST Year B	10	11	12	13	14
Second Lesson	→Eph. 4:1-7, 11-16	→Eph. 4:17-24	→Eph. 4:30-5:2	→Eph. 5:15-20	→Eph. 5:21-31→
	Continues 8 weeks of readings, these last six mostly paraenetic (ethical) and ecclesiological.				
	→CL = 3:14-21	→4:1-6	→4:25-5:2		RC, v.32; E,CL, v.33
FIRST LESSON	CL continues 14 weeks of the epic story of David, as found in 1 and 2 Samuel, 1 Kings.				
	→2 Sam. 12:1-14	→2 Sam. 12:15b-24	→2 Sam. 18:1,5,9-15	→2 Sam. 18:24-33	→2 Sam. 23:1-17→
	Nathan's parable to David; "... you are the man"	David fasts, but Bathsheba's child dies; Solomon born	Absalom, David's rebel son, killed at the order of Joab	David informed by a Cushite and laments, "Absalom, my son!"	The last words of David, God's anointed
	2 Kings 4:42-44	**Exod. 16:2-15**	**1 Kings 19:4-8**	**Prov. 9:1-6**	**Josh. 24:1-2a, 14-18**
	Enough food through Elisha	Israel complains in the wilderness.	Elijah flees into the wilderness, ready to die under a broom tree.	Dame Wisdom's invitation: "Come eat of my bread, drink of my wine..." To eat bread = receive wisdom or revelation	The tribes at Shechem pledge to serve the Lord who brought them up from slavery in Egypt. "Choose, this day..."
	OR **2 Kings 2:1-15** Elisha succeeds Elijah	God will send bread from heaven.	Fed by an angel, he journeys 40 days to Horeb. (E has Deut. 8:1-10)		
	OR **Exod. 24:3-11** Israel at Sinai, Mosaic covenant; the elders see God, eat and drink	The "manna miracle"			
GOSPEL FOR DAY	→John 6:1-15	→John 6:24-35	→John 6:41-51	→John 6:51-58	→John 6:60-69
	Johannine insertion for 5 weeks into the "Year of Mark." 6:51 is an overlay, read twice.				
OT and Gospel Themes	Feeding of 5000 Jesus: prophet king? Jesus withdraws (E has Mark 6:45-52)	At Capernaum. "Signs." The "work of God" = faith. Manna in the wilderness. "I am the bread of life"	The Jews complain. "Drawn by the Father." To believe = to have eternal life. "I am the living bread"	The Jews dispute "eating his flesh." True food/drink, abiding, living forever. How much is "eucharistic"?	A "hard teaching." Jesus' words = spirit and life. Many do not believe and turn away. Peter's confession
	Food and drink as a vehicle for God; miracle	Manna/bread; Christology and faith	"I am..." (vv. 35, 41, 51). Belief as response	Wisdom and Word as bread and drink	Offense at Jesus or faith?

4

PENTECOST Year B	15	16	17	18	19
Second Lesson	Eph. 6:10-20	James 1:17-27	James 2:1-5,14-18	James 3:16-4:6	James 4:7-12
		Five or four weeks for paraenesis from a NT "wisdom book."			
		2:1-5	2:14-18	3:16-4:3	5:1-6
FIRST LESSON	Ordo: James 1:17-27				
	CL concludes David saga	CL inserts four weeks of OT wisdom literature			
	1 Kings 2:1-4, 10-12	Prov. 2:1-8	Prov. 22:1...9	Job 28:20-28	Job 42:1-6
	David's charge to Solomon, a "farewell speech"	Heed wisdom, obtain knowledge of God	Wisdom sayings on wealth and justice	Whence wisdom? – from God, to fear the Lord	Job's submission to God in dust and ashes
	Deut. 4:1...8 (9)	Isa. 35:4-7a	Isa. 50:4-10	Wisd. 2:12-20	Num. 11:4...29
	Obedience to God's Torah; blessing from God's "canonical" word	The deaf will hear, the speechless sing, upon return from exile	Third "servant song": the obedient teacher will be vindicated	God's righteous "child" will be vindicated OR Jer. 11:18-20 The prophets lament, opposed but trusting	The spirit of God comes upon the 70 elders but also upon Eldad and Medad in the camp
GOSPEL FOR DAY	Mark 7:1-8, 14-15, 21-23	Mark 7:31-37	Mark 8:27-35 (38)	Mark 9:30-37	Mark 9:38-50
	The commandment of God in contrast to human precepts; what comes out of a person defiles – words or foods.	Jesus heals a deaf man with impaired speech. The crowd ignores the order (messianic secret) not to tell it.	Peter confesses Jesus as messiah, but Jesus teaches a suffering Son of Man to disciples who misunderstand.	Second passion prediction. The messianic secret and dull disciples. Receiving children and those whom God sends.	Jesus refuses to curb an exorcist not of "our group." Rigorous self-discipline for disciples.
OT and Gospel Themes	Clean / unclean in God's will for life	The power of the eschatological age of God	Proper Christology and discipleship	Discipleship as proper Christology and response	God works beyond "official" structures. Sacrifice for the kingdom

Introduction and Abbreviations

An overview of readings for Pentecost 10 through 19 in Year B is given in the chart on pp. 4–5. The lines indicating connections reflect the principles of the Roman Catholic *Ordo Lectionem Missae* (1969) and subsequent versions in the Episcopal, Lutheran, and other churches in North America (referred to by the abbreviations RC, E, L, and CL [Common Lectionary]). See pp. 12, 18, and 30 below. Commentaries and other helps are cited by author and series using the following abbreviations:

AB	Anchor Bible (Garden City, N.Y.: Doubleday).
ABD	*The Anchor Bible Dictionary*, ed. D. N. Freedman (New York: Doubleday, 1992), 6 vols.
ACNT	Augsburg Commentary on the New Testament (Minneapolis: Augsburg).
CEV	*Bible for Today's Family*: Contemporary English Version (New York: American Bible Society, 1991).
EKK	Evangelisch-katholischer Kommentar zum Neuen Testament (Zürich: Benziger Verlag: Neukirchener-Vluyn: Neukirchener Verlag).
HNTC	Harper's New Testament Commentaries (San Francisco: Harper & Row).
Int	Interpretation (Atlanta, Louisville: John Knox).
NICNT	New International Commentary on the New Testament (Grand Rapids: Wm. B. Eerdmans).
NICOT	New International Commentary on the Old Testament (Grand Rapids: Wm. B. Eerdmans).
NIGTC	The New International Greek Testament Commentary (Grand Rapids: Wm. B. Eerdmans).
NJBC	*The New Jerome Biblical Commentary*, ed. R. A. Brown, J. A. Fitzmyer, and R. L. Murphy (Englewood Cliffs, N.J.: Prentice Hall, 1990).
OTL	Old Testament Library (Philadelphia: Westminster).
TINT	E. Schweizer, *A Theological Introduction to the New Testament* (Nashville: Abingdon, 1991).
VU	J. Reumann, *Variety and Unity in New Testament Thought* (New York: Oxford Univ. Press, 1991).
WBC	Word Biblical Commentary (Waco, Texas: Word Books).

Tenth Sunday after Pentecost

Lutheran	Roman Catholic	Episcopal	Common Lectionary
Exod. 24:3-11	2 Kings 4:42-44	2 Kings 2:1-15	2 Sam. 12:1-14
Eph. 4:1-7, 11-16	Eph. 4:1-6	Eph. 4:1-7, 11-16	Eph. 3:14-21
John 6:1-15	John 6:1-15	Mark 6:45-52	John 6:1-15

FIRST LESSON

Each of the four lectionaries goes its own way in the OT reading to be paired with the feeding of the five thousand (John 6:1-15). Originally the *Ordo* assigned a brief passage in 2 Kings about Elisha feeding a hundred people and having food left over. The L choice from Exodus 24 appoints a text employed by the *Ordo* for Corpus Christi Sunday in Year B (and hence not in Protestant readings; cf. R. Fuller's comment in *Preaching the New Lectionary* [Collegeville, Minn.: Liturgical Press, 1974], 385–86). Lutherans added to vv. 3-8, about the ratification of the covenant, vv. 9-11 about elders of Israel beholding God and eating and drinking on the heights of Sinai. The E reading (*2 Kings 2:1-15*) is the dramatic narrative about Elisha persistently following Elijah until the latter ascends into heaven and his mantle falls to Elisha. This splendid story, not assigned in the *Ordo* but used in L at the Transfiguration, Year B, is harder to relate to John 6, unless Jesus is thought of as a "new Elisha" (cf. 2 Kings 4:42-44), a typology less likely here than one about the prophet like Moses of Deut. 18:15, 18. In E, it goes with Jesus' walking on the water, *after* the feeding, read last week (Mark 6:30-44). Elijah parts the Jordan, Jesus rules the sea.

The CL reading, *2 Sam. 12:1-14*, on Nathan's parable to King David and its blunt critique, "You are the man!" continues the fourteen Sundays of narrative about David, from the week after Trinity Sunday through Pentecost 15. If a preacher has been following these epic selections from 1 and 2 Samuel, she or he is well advised to continue with 2 Sam. 12:1-14, and/or to make provision to follow up the next two weeks with the effects on the house of Israel of David's sin with Bathsheba. There are no particular links intended with the Gospel for the day; in this revision of the *Ordo*, the OT speaks in its own right. The tension between David's roles as greedy oppressor and as king administering justice provides the stuff for depicting messy life and tensions today. The "fourfold" restitution

PENTECOST 2, SERIES B

for a lamb (Exod. 22:1) may point to four judgments in David's "own house" (12:11)—Bathsheba's child, Tamar, Amnon, and Absalom; but P. K. McCarter, Jr. *II Samuel* (AB 9, [1984]: 294, 299) prefers "sevenfold" in the Greek.

2 Kings 4:42-44 can best be used to reinforce elements in the miracle story in John 6: Food is brought to a "man of God," here from "first fruits" of the grain harvest. The amount is specified, and someone (a servant here) objects that it is insufficient, but the prophet forges ahead and there are leftovers. Both stories feature generosity (4:42a; 6:9a) and doubt (4:43a; 6:6, 9b). There is some question whether the Elisha story really depicts a miracle (twenty loaves plus grain for only one hundred persons), but there has been a hint of famine (v. 38) and the account means it to be in accord with a "word of the Lord." See v. 43b for the "Thus-says-the-Lord" promise and emphasis on it at the end of v. 44. Promise fulfilled!

Exodus 24:3-11 places the unusual account about eating in God's presence (vv. 9-11) within a covenant context. The account of the Sinai covenant runs on from 19:1-8 (read at Vigil of Pentecost and 4 Pentecost A). Here in chap. 24, covenant ratification occurs first by a sprinkling of sacrificial blood (vv. 3-8) and secondly by a covenant meal (Exod. 18:12). While two sources seem involved (vv. 3-8 Elohist; vv. 1-2, 9-11 possibly Yahwist) and the first part deals with all the people and the latter verses with seventy-three leaders, the total passage presents reception of God's words (the Ten Commandments, and ordinances) so as to emphasize obedience (vv. 3b, 7) and communion (vv. 10-11). To "see" God is not, however, characteristic of biblical revelation (cf. 33:20), and 10b suggests the elders did not see God's throne (as in Isaiah 6) but only the lapis lazuli platform for it. They did not "eat God" or even "with God," they *and* God; but they eat and drink in the divine presence. In John 6, five thousand people (not just leaders) are fed, not just in the presence of Jesus but also by Jesus, who reveals the Father (6:27, 40, 46; 10:30).

SECOND LESSON: EPHESIANS 4:1-7, 11-16

The seven (RC) or eight weeks of lectionary readings from Ephesians continue during Pentecost 10 through 15 with excerpts from chaps. 4–6. (The CL is a week behind, this Sunday and next.) Most of this material is parenetic or ethical instruction and depends on the indicative statements in chaps. 1–3 about what God has done in Christ to effect redemption. In 4:1 the word *therefore* points to this shift toward the implications of redemption for conduct (cf. Rom. 12:1). Actually, much of the "doctrinal" portion in chaps. 1–3 is cast as praise of God (1:6, 12, 14; 3:21), and 4:4-6 and 4:7-13 contain indicative statements, from which imperatives are drawn (4:1b-3,14-15). Such requests, signaled by the verb "I beg" in v. 1 ("beseech, exhort"), are also characteristic of papyrus letters. That Paul writes as a prisoner in Christ's service (4:1; cf. 3:1; 6:20) heightens the significance of what the apostle asks. Although some commentators, such as Markus Barth (AB 34, 34A, 1974), defend authorship by Paul, most regard him as implied author, while the real author is a follower of Paul, in western Asia Minor, about A.D. 90 (so recently W. Taylor, ACNT; R. P. Martin, Int; R. Schnackenburg, EKK; A. T. Lincoln, WBC). Colossians, especially 3:12-15, provides material here reworked (e.g., the three emphases in 4:2, "humility, gentleness, and patience," come from a list of five positive qualities at Col. 3:12). The immediate aims in 4:1-16 are to urge unity and a way of life that accords with our calling into Christ's body (4:4, 12, 16). (For recent assessments of Ephesians as a whole, see P. J. Kobelski, *NJBC* #55; Reumann, *VU* 105, 114–23; V. P. Furnish, *ABD* 2:535–42; Schweizer, *TINT* 95–98 [#18].)

The initial admonitions call for "every effort" to "bear with" fellow saints—that is, Christian neighbors with whom we may have all too much contact, toward whom it is a challenge to keep on expressing self-effacing love—and to maintain (not create) God-given unity (vv. 2-3). The ethical exhortation is then interrupted by a list in vv. 4-6 of seven unities that comprise a sort of Apostles' Creed in reverse: church, Spirit, and (eschatological) hope (v. 4); Lord (Jesus Christ), faith (in Christ), and baptism (into Christ, 1 Cor. 12:12-13; less clearly, Christ's death for us, cf. Mark 10:38) (v. 5); and one God, the Father (v. 6). The RC selection of 4:1-6 thus focuses on exhortation and credo, above all on "calling" (vv. 1, 4); similarly CL for Pentecost 11.

By adding vv. 7 and 11-16, the L and E pericope goes on, with Ephesians, to assert how "each of us was given grace" by Christ (v. 7) and how Christ gave (or appointed) leaders for the body of Christ (v. 11), to build up (vv. 12, 16) that body and bring all to the appointed goals: unity of faith, maturity, and growth in love (vv. 12-16). The author's difficult use in 4:8-10 of Ps. 68:19 (in a modified version of the LXX) is thereby omitted, though its verb "he gave gifts" is the basis for the theme of "Christ's gift" in v. 7 and "the gifts he gave" in v. 11. The reference in v. 9 is not to incarnation or descent into Hades but to a salvation victory in Christ's reascent into the heavens (cf. Phil. 2:9-11).

Christ's gift of leaders to the church involves apostles, prophets, evangelists, and shepherd-teachers (v. 11; cf. 1 Cor. 12:28). The three phrases in v. 12 have in recent decades commonly been interpreted to mean that these leaders in the word equip all Christians who then do "the work of ministry," and so build up Christ's body (RSV, NRSV). More recently there has been a tendency to restore the comma after "saints," as in KJV, so that it is the leaders who do "the work of ministry" (e.g., Lincoln, 253; J. N. Collins, *Diakonia* [Oxford Univ. Press, 1990], 233–34). In that case, "every ligament" mentioned in v. 16 may then refer to the church leaders (cf. Col. 2:19; Lincoln, 263, 266). But for all the emphasis in these verses on church leadership as Christ-given, such an interpretation overlooks the point that ministry or service occurs in the world, a cosmic emphasis involving every believer (4:15, 25; 5:8-11; 6:12). But a Catholic/Protestant tension exists over how much stress is to be placed on "church office" here (cf. E. Schweizer, in Schnackenburg, EKK 191–92).

Even more significant are the eschatological limitation in v. 13 on ecclesial possibilities here and now (unity and perfection are future); the warning against crafty schemes in doctrine in v. 14; the pointed motto in v. 15, "speaking the truth in love," and the growth motif ("into Christ, from whom . . ."). Overall, the emphasis is ecclesiological, not individual, growth. The church as "one new humanity" (2:15, *anthrōpos*) looks to the Perfect Man (4:13 *anēr*), Christ, as measure (4:7, 16 *metron*) of maturity.

For the next six weeks a series of sermons on Ephesians 4–6 is possible. This Sunday the theme could be church and ministry, set within creed (or faith) and exhortation, for life together and community growth in love and truth.

GOSPEL: JOHN 6:1-15

At the point where Mark would follow last week's reading (6:30-34) with an account of the feeding of the five thousand (6:35-44), the *Ordo* and related lectionaries substitute the Johannine version of this miracle. For the next four weeks John 6 will be read, excerpts from the discourse on the bread of life. Only on Pentecost 15 will the readings return to Mark, at 7:1. The insertion of five weeks from John 6 was made, ostensibly, to piece out the shorter Mark and get in more of John (usually read on the Sundays of Easter), so as to give the Fourth Gospel proportional time. The shift also involves material that traditionally has been taken in John 6 as eucharistic; the *Ordo* is readings for mass, though not every other church employing a version of its Three-Year Lectionary features Eucharist every Sunday. The preacher is well advised to let the texts themselves set the themes. They do not always say what tradition has thought.

The feeding of the five thousand is the only miracle recounted in all four Gospels. The lectionary also assigns the Matthean version (14:13-21) in Year A. The feeding of the four thousand (in Mark 8:1-10; par. Matt. 15:32-39) is not used in the Three-Year Lectionary. While comparison of the six accounts is interesting (see R. M. Brown, *John*, AB 29 [1966]: 236–44), it is not in itself material for sermons. We concentrate on John, but recall that the congregation heard Matthew 14 about a year ago. As transition from Mark, one should stick to the (common) miracle story, emphasizing Johannine features in 6:1-15, without anticipating what will be done and said in 6:16-71. This much may be anticipated, however: 6:1-15 is the first of two nature miracles (the second, 6:16-21, walking on the sea, will not be read in the lectionary, though its Markan version, 6:45-52, is, in E). Dialogue will follow on meaning (6:22-31), then Jesus' long discourse (vv. 32-59). The lectionary takes up only the bread-manna part (24ff.). (On John generally, cf. P. Perkins, *NJBC* #61; *VU* 63–70; R. Kysar, *ABD* 3:912–31; *TINT* 149–56 [#29]).

A large crowd follows Jesus, for the sake of his miracles, to the other side of the Sea of Galilee. (In Mark and Matthew this is to a deserted spot on its east side. Presumably this is true also in John 6:1 NRSV, but there is a textual variant about "the region of Tiberias" [not "Tiberius"; cf. 6:23]; later they cross from the east side [or from Tiberias] to Capernaum, vv. 17, 24.) The word *sign* (*sēmeion*) for miracle is Johannine. A first example occurred at 2:11 (water into wine at Cana; cf. 2:18, 23; 3:2). A second sign is recounted and numbered at 4:48, 54 (official's son at Capernaum). It will be a key term in chap. 6 (vv. 2, 14, 26, 30, Jesus' "third" sign, though no further numbering follows after "second" in 4:54).

"The mountain" (6:3) is not further identified, and one should be wary of conflating it with the mountain for the sermon in Matthew 5–7 or with Sinai, in the absence of any clue from John. In 6:15 Jesus "withdrew again to the mountain." It is unclear whether he had come downslope at some point or now retreated up into its heights. Or have we two sources? To sit (with the disciples, 6:3) is the position for a Jewish teacher, but no instruction is presented here. John alone tells us it was Passover time, which is part of his habit of dating events by Jewish festivals (2:13, 23; 5:1; 10:22; 11:55) and not necessarily a last supper/eucharistic reference, any more than it is here a reference to Jesus' death at Passover. John does not tell us, however, that the hour was late in the day (cf. Mark 6:35). The dialogue where the disciples (here Philip) are tested to find a solution for the crowd's hunger (6:5-8) is similar to Mark 6:37. Another similarity is the presence of a lad with fish and bread; here Andrew locates him (6:8). In the Fourth Gospel Jesus more clearly takes the initiative (v. 5b). The grass (v. 10) is a sign of spring (Passover time).

The actions of taking the food, thanking God, and distributing the food (6:11) are common to any Jewish (and many Greek) meals, a pattern to which the last supper conforms, not a sign of a "eucharist." The Synoptic detail of "breaking the bread" (a practical necessity) is unmentioned, nor is the disciples' helping to distribute. John means the event as a miraculous feeding where people got as much real food (from the limited but typical menu of the day) as they wanted (v. 12). The miraculous nature of the multiplication of food is underscored in vv. 12-13. As in the Synoptics, twelve baskets are specified, but nothing is made of the number, and the fish fragments are not mentioned. The miracle story is being told for what will follow about bread (e.g., 6:23, 26, 32). The phrase "so that nothing may be lost" (v. 12) may point to v. 39 (that Jesus "should lose nothing of all that [= all whom] God has given me"), or to v. 27 (on the importance of food from God).

The crowd reaction in John 6:14, a feature in miracle stories, is unparalleled in the Synoptics. The people think Jesus is "the prophet" of Deut. 18:15-18, like Moses (cf. 7:40; Acts 3:22). So strong is their feeling that Jesus fears they will try by force to make him king. That would mean a Zealot messiah, such as Peter apparently looked for (Mark 8:29; see Pentecost 17). Jesus avoids all such ideas by withdrawing in solitude.

What to preach? First, the miraculous power of God at work through Jesus, in signs of the kingdom. Second, Jesus as the prophet like Moses, but not a Zealot (nationalist, military) messiah. Reflection of Zealot ideas may also be seen in the epistles for Pentecost 18 and 19 and the Gospel for Pentecost 17. Third, food as a vehicle for God's presence. Fourth, from the OT: the RC lectionary (2 Kings 4) presents an Elisha parallel also underscoring God's power to multiply resources. The choice of Exodus 24 apparently links seeing (God) with eating (6:2, 5, 14 do use "see"). Excellent OT texts are found in E and CL. But none of these can be shown to have been in John's ken. More pertinent might be the messianic banquet theme (Isa. 25:6-12; 65:13), for the crowd now; for Jesus, as future fulfillment.

The next four weeks' Gospels lend themselves to a sermon sequence. If one reading from John 6 is expounded, all should be: not just Pentecost 13, seemingly on the Eucharist, but also 11-12 and the climactic 14. We have discourse and dialogue begun with the narrative in 6:1-15. The drama, as Dorothy Sayers once suggested, is in the dogma or teaching, not just the narrative. Jesus is a teacher and an event.

In the lectionary, the Gospel reading for the day is foundational. The first lesson (OT) is meant to relate to this Gospel passage as background, reinforcement, or contrast. The second reading provides in-sequence selections, usually from a NT epistle. Connections between OT and Gospel lessons are to be assumed, for better or for worse. Links with the epistle come from the happy unities of Scripture, as brought out by biblical theology, not necessarily from the design of the lectionary.

Eleventh Sunday after Pentecost

Lutheran	Roman Catholic	Episcopal	Common Lectionary
Exod. 16:2-15	Exod. 16:2-4, 12-15	Exod. 16:2-4, 9-15	2 Sam. 12:15b-24
Eph. 4:17-24	Eph. 4:17, 20-24	Eph. 4:17-25	Eph. 4:1-6
John 6:24-35	John 6:24-35	John 6:24-35	John 6:24-35

FIRST LESSON: EXODUS 16:2-15

This account about the Israelites' complaining in the wilderness until God sends bread (manna) and meat (quails) to assuage their hunger is assigned in all lectionaries based on the Roman *Ordo*, as a background counterpart to Jesus' discourse in Capernaum on "bread from heaven." The link to the Gospel reading is that a summary of 16:4 and 16:15 is quoted at John 6:31, God "gave them bread from heaven to eat."

The CL (*2 Sam. 12:15b-24*) continues the David saga with the sequel to last week's reading. Today's concerns David's vigil of fasting and prayer for the child Bathsheba bore him. In accord with Nathan's word (read last week), "The Lord struck the child" with illness (2 Sam. 12:15b). David persists in his importuning for a week, but to no avail. The child dies. Then, to the surprise of his servants (vv. 21-23), David realistically returns to the business of life, cleaned up, eating, and consoling Bathsheba. The note of good news is that she becomes pregnant again and gives birth to a son who will be the great ruler Solomon (cf. also 11:27). When to grieve and plead with a gracious and judging God, and when to eat and make love and worship a gracious and judging God are dramatically portrayed. David had confessed his sin and been forgiven (12:13), but at a cost—to others. For various political and theological judgments within this account, see McCarter (AB 9, 1984), 301–9, or A. A. Anderson, *2 Samuel* (WBC 11, 1989), 163–66.

Exodus 16 recounts the second of three tests for Israel in the wilderness (the others are 15:22-27, murmuring about bitter water at Marah; 17:1-7, thirst at Meribah). Here at a place called Sin they murmur (NRSV regularly has "complain") against Moses and Aaron (16:2) and ultimately against God (v. 8). Better to have remained well-fed slaves in Egypt (v. 3)! God responds, not truculently but with a generous offer of "bread from heaven" each day, but will test them through an order to gather twice as much on the sixth day, for sabbath. (By omitting vv. 5-11, RC and E skip over the content of the instructions to be followed and over a certain repetitiveness as Moses and Aaron repeat to the Israelites what God had told them. Emphasis in vv. 7 and 10 on the glory of the Lord who speaks and acts is thus also omitted.) The promise of meat at twilight and of bread in the morning (v. 12) is literally fulfilled through quails and manna. Both gifts can be explained naturally: exhausted migratory birds and honeylike secretions from insects on tamarisk trees. Their continued, regular appearance is phenomenal, however.

This story is also told in Numbers 11, with a different pattern. There, God is angry; it is the "rabble" who "crave" meat. The quails come as a result of complaints about manna, but a plague results from eating their meat). Psalm 78:17-31 is similar (cf. also Ps. 105:40). John 6 may also be aware of these several OT treatments. The emphasis is on manna as bread "from heaven." Anyone preaching on Exodus 16 ought to pick up the themes of murmuring, divine response, and testing, all pertinent to John 6. The manna story has several NT interpretations, however (cf. Jesus' temptation over bread; 1 Cor. 10:3; Rev. 2:17). See B. Childs, *Exodus* (OTL, 1974), 295–304, for a history of applications, including a warning that extending the manna theme too exclusively to "heavenly food" and the Eucharist has resulted in a separation from its OT base, God's concern for *physical* hunger. As T. E. Fretheim puts it (*Exodus* [Int, 1991], 181–87), a "food crisis" leads to a "faith crisis," which is met by God in daily life, one day at a time.

SECOND LESSON: EPHESIANS 4:17-24

At last in these verses begin the ethical admonitions toward which Paul pointed at 3:1 and 4:1. "This," in 4:17, on which Paul insists, rests upon prior assertions about God's work in Christ to save (2:4-10) and looks forward for content to 4:17b and the triple assertions of vv. 22-24 ("put away . . . be renewed . . . clothe yourselves"). That the prisoner-apostle (4:1) speaks "in the Lord" (4:17) lends authority. Paul addresses here a broad Christian audience (us included), not just Ephesian believers (for whom v. 21 would be odd, since Acts 19:10 says he spent over two years with them, teaching). The immediate aim of the passage is to help saints, who are in danger of amnesia about their faith and life, "walk" (live, conduct themselves, 2:2, 10; 4:1, 17) in a renewed Christian way (cf. also 5:2, 8, 15 for this theme of how one lives in the Lord). The call is not just for an individual to have a "closer walk with Jesus" but for a renewed one, morally and together with other Christians, in the world.

The passage is at several points dependent on Col. 3:5-10 for key phrases like "old self/new self" (*anthrōpos*, vv. 22, 24), but often with a twist. Of five earthly vices mentioned in Col. 3:5, for example, only one is repeated at Eph. 4:19 (NRSV "greedy"). The contrast in Col. 3:1-2 between "things above" and earthly things becomes one in Ephesians between Gentiles and Christians (4:17-21). The verses admonish believers not to live as the Gentiles do (vv. 17-20) but to be renewed in Christian truth (vv. 21-24). The RC pericope omits vv. 18-19 on Gentile alienation from God, though these verses provide the foil to what those in Christ once were and ought now to be. The E reading adds v. 25 (also found the next week in CL) about putting off falsehood and speaking truth because "we are members of one another" (cf. Rom. 12:5). The latter phrase again introduces the communal theme that runs through the chapter.

The two segments present a past/present contrast. Formerly (vv. 17-20) those addressed were mired in emptiness, moral blackout, insensitivity, and alienation from all divine life, ignorant about God, with resulting impurity of life. Not to know God shows up in the gross ways people live. But now (21ff.), having learned Christ (a person, not just a subject), they are to put off old ways (v. 22) and put on the new, godlike self (v. 24). Somewhat surprising—but realistic—is the way the admonitions are addressed to people who have already heard Christian teaching and have been baptized (cf. 4:5); "put away" and "clothe yourselves" (vv. 22, 24) are commonly taken as imagery from a baptismal ritual (though evidence for reclothing with white robes is available only in the second or third century). Already here (and in Col. 3:9-10) such imagery has been cast in moral terms: One puts away past lusts and puts on righteousness and holiness.

Three points are addressed to members of Christ's body. These may be taken as imperatives (as in RSV, "put off . . . be renewed . . . put on") or taken with "you were taught to" (v. 21; so NRSV, supplied in v. 22) or as the content of "the truth in Jesus." The first and last admonitions are single decisive actions, as in baptism: "put off your old nature . . . put on the new nature" (RSV). By repeating the statement long after the baptismal ceremony, Paul is urging implementation in daily life of the convert's shift to Christ. While for reasons of inclusive language recent translators avoid the terms "old man" and "new man," terms like "nature" and even "self" may blur the personal yet corporate sense of (old) Adam and (new) Christ. The middle assertion, with its sense of repeated action, becomes the decisive one: keep on being renewed in the spirit of your minds (v. 23). While this involves the Spirit (3:16), here in 4:20-24 Christ-terms are used to describe the remaking of the inner person.

This process, a continual actualizing of what believers are to be in life, lays considerable emphasis on the mind (v. 23, cf. v. 17); truth and learning through hearing in contrast to ignorance (vv. 18, 20, 21); teaching (v.

21), and hence teachers (= the leaders in 4:11-12). Behind the "new person" (v. 24) lies a story: Adam and Eve were created in the likeness of God (Gen. 1:26, 27), which was lost. As in Col. 1:15, it is here understood that only Jesus Christ is then "the image of the invisible God." But now those united with Christ (in baptism) are renewed in the Creator's image (Col. 3:10). In such persons the epistle sees a "third race," beyond Jews and Gentiles (Eph. 2:6-7, 12, 15b-16; cf. 1 Cor. 10:32).

The passage can be preached as ethics (but there is little specific content) or with an ecclesial note (v. 25b). But this may be the place to set forth Ephesians' "anthropology" for people today: the human situation as a contrast between life without God and life in Christ; as a decisive step (of coming to faith and baptism) and a continuing renewal, one that involves the word in teaching. The gospel calls people to become in daily life what they already are in Christ and to walk to a different drummer and accept different norms than their unbelieving neighbors do.

GOSPEL: JOHN 6:24-35

The lectionary here reflects familiar Johannine devices, to relate an event (the feeding miracle, 6:1-13) to a discourse by Jesus (6:32-51), with interruptions and misunderstandings by "the Jews" at 6:34, 41-42, and 52. Compare the blind man healed in 9:1-7 and the light-of-the-world discourse in 8:12ff. (cf. 9:5). The lectionary omits 6:16-21, in part because the Matthean version (Matt. 14:22-32) has been read in Year A (Pentecost 12). Any exposition of v. 24 may need to allude to vv. 22-23, how the crowd at the feeding came along to Capernaum (vv. 17, 21). What follows is often called Jesus' "Capernaitic discourse." Once the crowd finds Jesus there (cf. 6:59, which makes the site, at least for the immediately preceding verses, specifically the synagogue in Capernaum), they naturally ask, "When did you come here?" (v. 25). They are unaware of the incident at sea (vv. 17-21, 22b; it is unclear whether Jesus finished the trip by boat). Disciples go unmentioned in the story until 6:60, 66; "the twelve," until v. 67. The general sequence in John 6:1-25 follows Mark: the five thousand fed (Mark 6:31-44), walking on the sea (Mark 6:45-52), and a bit later a dispute with the Jews (in Mark 7:1, specifically Pharisees and scribes from Jerusalem).

Two factors complicate interpretation of John 6:25ff.: First, Peder Borgen (*Bread from Heaven*, [Leiden: Brill, 1965]) has argued that 6:31-58 represents a unified midrash, or exposition of Scripture. Verse 31 provides the basic text (= Exod. 16:4, 15; see also Ps. 78:22-25). The alternate theory that Jesus is following a synagogue lectionary which involves Exodus 16, Numbers 11, Genesis 2–3, and Isaiah 54–55 is unlikely. The midrashic-techniques view is widely accepted, though other factors are also involved.

Second, only in 6:51b-58 does the chapter make overt reference to the Lord's Supper ("gnawing" Jesus' "flesh" and drinking blood; see Pentecost 13). How much does this note spill over into the discourse in 6:31ff.? X. Léon-Dufour, S.J., *Sharing the Eucharistic Bread* (New York: Paulist, 1987), 252–72, has shown how all of John 6 can be given either a "spontaneous" reading by "Christians who regularly celebrate the Eucharist," so that all is eucharistic; or a "critical" reading so that even 6:51-58 can be read noneucharistically. He concludes with a "symbolic" reading to show how all of chap. 6 can be read both sacramentally and as a discourse about believing.

John's emphasis on faith will stand out in 6:29 (cf. vv. 30, 35, 36, 40, 47, 64, 65, 69). The related theme is Christology. Jesus' statement in v. 35, "I am the bread of life," will be the offense (cf. 41). Hence Markus Barth, *Rediscovering the Lord's Supper* (Atlanta: John Knox, 1988), 83–84, has listed four schools of thought on John 6: (*a*) vv. 27-51a are taken "spiritually," vv. 51b-58 "eucharistically"; (*b*) all these verses are sacramental; (*c*) all the verses are both spiritual and sacramental (Léon-Dufour); (*d*) vv. 32-58 describe "the faith relation to Christ" (Augustine; M. Barth). (Cf. G. R. Beasley-Murray, *John* [WBC 36, 1987], 98–99). We shall treat vv. 27-51 as a discourse on faith and Christ, with the Eucharist alluded to only on a subordinate level, and that perhaps more from the perspective of some readers than of the biblical author or source. (Cf. R. Schnackenburg, *John* [New York: Crossroad] 2 [1982]: 36–37, 45; R. Brown [AB 29:272–74], the Eucharist is a secondary theme in vv. 35-50, become primary in 51-58.)

The crowd in 6:25, though earlier having apparently regarded Jesus as the prophet like Moses and a potential anointed king (6:14-15), now addresses him simply as "rabbi." They continue to follow him just for his miracles (6:2), Jesus charges (v. 26). Instead of food to fill their bellies, he counsels, "work for . . . the food that endures for eternal life" (v. 27). This the Son of Man will give, on whom "the Father has set his seal." While "Son of Man" can mean simply "I" (cf. 4:14, where Jesus says to the Samaritan woman, "I will give" water so that people may never thirst), the term from the outset in John points to one who comes from the world above and who will return there (1:51)—but who will also be "lifted up" (on the cross, 3:14; 8:28). It is thus less veiled in meaning than in the Synoptics.

The "seal" is a confirmation of approval by God but also the giving of divine power for Jesus' work (cf. 3:33 NRSV note, in the context of 3:31-35); he has the words of life (3:34; 6:63b, 68b). God has "sanctified and sent" him (10:36) to die and bring life. Jesus' solemn assertion (beginning in Greek *amēn, amēn,* 6:26; NRSV "Very truly") is the statement in 6:27b.

The Jews misunderstand and ask what they must do. In his response, again employing the root "to work" (five times in vv. 27-30), Jesus says ironically that there is only one "work" God wills and accomplishes in people, that they believe and continue to have faith in the one whom God sent. The Jews demand a sign or work from Jesus. They set the stage for his discussion by proudly quoting the Exodus text about Moses giving their ancestors "bread from heaven to eat" (see OT lesson).

Following midrashic techniques, Jesus in v. 32 makes three corrections: not "Moses" but "my Father"; not "gave" but "gives"; not manna but the "true" bread from heaven. Now comes the bridge to Christology (v. 33): "the bread of God is that which comes down from heaven and gives life to the world," but, as the NRSV note brings out, the ambiguous Greek (for the masculine noun "bread") could also mean ". . . is he who comes . . . and gives life. . . ." The Jews, of course, want such bread "always." The clinching comment is, "I am the bread of life . . . ," one of the "I am" (christological) claims in the Fourth Gospel (8:12; 9:5; 10:7, 9; 10:11, 14; 11:25; 14:6; 15:1, 5). In 6:35b Jesus begins to explicate it with a promise: Whoever comes to Jesus and believes will never hunger or thirst. The addition of "thirst" (not from the feeding miracle) may allude to 4:14 or to water as well as manna in the wilderness (Num. 20:2-11). Hunger and thirst often go together (Isa. 49:10a). But the ultimate background seems to be in Prov. 9:5, where Wisdom invites the simple to eat her bread and drink her wine, a metaphor for receiving her instruction (cf. also Sir. 24:21). Of that, more later.

Jesus' challenge is to believe in him. To believe is to receive the true bread, himself. Faith and Christology are thus set forth in 6:27-35.

In the rubrics of some churches if one lesson is omitted, it is the second reading. In the chart on pp. 4–5, the OT and Gospel readings are set next to each other to facilitate seeing lines of linkage that are to be expected. In the exegesis the three are taken up in their normal order of reading: OT, Epistle, Gospel. Sermon series can be proposed on a Gospel sequence like Pentecost 10–14 or 16–19, but from the OT usually only in the Common Lectionary (Pentecost 10–15).

Twelfth Sunday after Pentecost

Lutheran	Roman Catholic	Episcopal	Common Lectionary
1 Kings 19:4-8	1 Kings 19:4-8	Deut. 8:1-10	2 Sam. 18:1, 5, 9-15
Eph. 4:30—5:2	Eph. 4:30—5:2	Eph. 4:30—5:2	Eph. 4:25—5:2
John 6:41-51	John 6:41-51	John 6:37-51	John 6:35, 41-51

FIRST LESSON: 1 KINGS 19:4-8

This brief segment in the Elijah cycle, where the prophet, despondent in the wilderness, casts himself down under a broom tree to die, is chosen to be read along with the Gospel lesson on the bread discourse in John 6 solely because here God, through an angel, provides cake and water to revive Elijah. The food strengthens him for a journey of forty days to Mount Horeb (Sinai). The lectionary takes this OT miracle typologically, as Fuller noted, "a type of holy communion considered as the food of pilgrims on their way to the mountain of God" (*Preaching*, 411).

The CL choice (*2 Sam. 18:1, 5, 9-15*) reflects an ecumenical effort to get away from such typology and give place to greater chunks of OT epic. In 2 Samuel 18 the story of God's judgment on the sin of David (with Bathsheba, see Pentecost 10) is continued with a second instance of retribution. Nathan's prophecy, "The child that is born to you shall die" (12:14), was carried out in last week's lesson; now Nathan's words that "the sword shall never depart from your house" (12:10) are fulfilled in the death by spearing of David's beloved son Absalom (18:9-15). Next week's reading will continue with David's poignant lament when he is finally informed of the death of his fair-haired heir. The lectionary includes only a bit of the setting (18:1, 5). The preacher will have to decide how much to present of Absalom's righteous rage over his half-sister's rape, his coup d'état against David, and the civil war that followed (2 Samuel 13–18). A character study is possible, in Absalom's ambition or in Joab's *Realpolitik* (14:1-23; 18:9-15); cf. Bible dictionaries.

The E assignment of *Deut. 8:1-10* is part of Moses' farewell address where Israel is reminded of God's "testing you" in the wilderness by "letting you hunger, then by feeding you with manna" (8:3). That phrase and the promise of a land "where you may eat bread without scarcity" (8:9) are the intended links to John 6. As with the L choice of Exodus 24 for Pentecost 10, this is a text used in the *Ordo* for Corpus Christi (Year A,

Deut. 8:2-3, 14b-16a) and thus available for Anglican use here. Lutherans assign Deut. 8:1-10 to Thanksgiving. The phrase in 8:3 ("not by bread alone") will remind listeners of Jesus' temptation in Matthew 4 and Luke 4 (Lent 1). **What of 1 Kings 19:4-8?** The prophet Elijah, flush with his triumph at Mount Carmel over the prophets of Baal and their subsequent massacre and a rain to break the drought (chap. 18), now finds himself on the run from the threats on his life by Queen Jezebel (19:1-3). Burned out, he flees in utter depression (see R. D. Nelson, *First and Second Kings* [Int 1987] 122–29, on psychological aspects). The theme of the life of a prophet of God runs through the account (vv. 2, 3, 4b; cf. 10, 14). The twofold dream epiphany (vv. 5-6, 7-8) has a certain parallelism with two earlier feedings of Elijah by God (17:3-6, 8-16). God's messenger arms Elijah for a journey that will prove tougher than the prophet is (cf. B. O. Long, *1 Kings*, Forms of Old Testament Literature 9 [Grand Rapids: Eerdmans, 1984], 196–204). The lectionary stops short, however, of the climax of Elijah's journey, the revelation and recommissioning at Horeb. The cake and jar of water attracted later typologists, who give them eucharistic overtones. A broader theme is Yahweh's care for those who remain faithful even in times of despair. Sustenance, however, is not enough (v. 6, to eat, drink, and lie down); there is a goal (vv. 7-8).

SECOND LESSON: EPHESIANS 4:30—5:2

Readings from Eph. 4:17-32, 5:15-21, and 6:10-17 were for centuries used in the Roman missal, Book of Common Prayer, and Lutheran lectionaries around St. Michael's Day (Pentecost 19–22) to stress practical aspects of faith and life. To the short reading in the *Ordo* (also L and E) of Eph. 4:30—5:2, about ethics for people who have Christ and the Spirit, CL has appended 4:25 (also in E last week) plus vv. 26-29. These verses provide a series of loosely structured sentences or admonitions: be truthful (v. 25; cf. Zech. 8:16); if angry (or disturbed, Ps. 4:5 NRSV), seek reconciliation the same day (vv. 26-27; cf. Matt. 5:22-24); instead of stealing, do honest work—and share with the needy (v. 28); utter no foul speech (or dirty badinage, 5:4; cf. Col. 3:8) or gossip, but instead "build up" (vv. 12, 16) the community (or faith, NRSV note) (v. 29)—say something constructive! The premise is startling: Gracious words (from Christians) bring grace to those who hear (v. 29). These varied exhortations provide further examples beyond the terse five verses that follow. Again Colossians is frequently a source (esp. Col. 3:8-14), but the Pauline teacher of the church who is writing here draws also on the OT (4:25, 26, above; 4:30 and 5:2, below).

Verse 30, about not grieving the Holy Spirit of God, seems abrupt, though the Spirit has been stressed at 4:3-4. There is a shift from a general structure in vv. 25-29 of negative, then positive injunction ("put away falsehood," "speak truth"), followed by motivation ("for we are members of one another," 4:25). Verse 30 alludes to Isa. 63:10 (the Israelites grieved Yahweh's holy spirit, so that God became their enemy). But the point must be supplied that for baptized children of God to do the things enumerated in vv. 25-29 or to continue in the characteristics of mind (like bitterness) and practices (like wrangling) that are listed in v. 31 will grieve God's Spirit, with which each Christian and the community have been "sealed" (at baptism; 1:13-14; cf. 2 Cor. 1:22; 5:5). The premise is "Spirit, church," therefore a certain kind of life-style. Moreover, v. 31 (with *kai* in Greek, a connective rare in Ephesians) begins a section that is both conclusion to 4:22-29 and basis for what follows. "So," we might render it, life in the Spirit is involved, pointing to "the day of redemption" or liberation, an inheritance already given but not yet at our disposal (1:14; 4:13).

To take v. 31 as an imperative ("Put away from you," NRSV) parallels it with 4:22 but misses the literal sense of the verb, "let (it) be put away," possibly a "divine passive" form (ACNT; i.e., put away by God) or overlooks a possible prayer form present here (as in Matt. 6:9-10; hence M. Barth, "shall be taken away from you" [AB 34A:522]). In any case, Spirit and believer are involved in a drama conveyed in terms from Col. 3:8: bitterness within a person bursts forth in wrath and anger (cf. 4:26), and the results are wrangling (shouting, quarreling) and slander (open abuse or vilification), together with all sorts of malice. From this, Lord, deliver! Instead believers should be kind (*chrēstoi*, possibly wordplay on "Christ" and "Christian"), warm-hearted, forgiving one another as Christ forgave each of them in making them part of the church community, the body of Christ.

This ethic is then escalated a final, daring notch: God's beloved children, living in love, are to be "imitators *of God*" (5:1, italics added). The idea of imitation comes from the Greek (*mimēsis*); Greek education sought a model, often in the teacher, who embodied ideals. Paul sometimes used the theme to help his Greek converts grapple concretely with the new faith and life in Christ (Phil. 3:17, Paul and others model what it means to be justified by faith and live accordingly, Phil. 3:8-16; he, in turn, reflects Christ, 1 Cor. 11:1). But who can imitate God? The OT only rarely has such ideas (e.g., Lev. 19:2; cf. 1 Pet. 1:15-16). In Hellenistic Judaism the notion was more common. Ephesians 5:1-2 clarifies for believers what would be incomprehensible and bad news for unbelievers by specifying imitation of God's love, *as revealed in Christ and his death* (to suggest its unique value, phrases are used from Ps. 40:6; Exod. 29:18; Lev. 2:9, 12).

The key is *as* Christ first loved us and *as* God has adopted us (Eph. 1:5). Therefore, walk in love like this! Husbands are to take special note (Eph. 5:25).

Our pericope lays bare the heart of morality for people who have received "truth in Jesus" (4:20-21, stressed by M. Barth [AB 34A:533–36]) and God's Holy Spirit (4:30, their "seal" or mark). This social ethics for their community life calls on them to be gracious, loving, even self-sacrificial. In a world where, then as now, people complained that all things remained as they were (2 Pet. 3:4), Christians are to be different from their neighbors. This does not stop the apostle, however, from borrowing phrases from the OT or topics like "imitation" from the Gentiles. But what gives the ethics its edge is the motivation ("as Christ loved") and the ecclesiology (a community of forgiven lovers).

GOSPEL: JOHN 6:41-51

The lectionary makes a good splice between 6:35, the end of last week's reading, and 6:41. In v. 35 Jesus made the claim to be the bread of life (repeated in vv. 41, 48, and 51), in whom, if people come and believe, they will never hunger. At this "the Jews began to complain" (v. 41). Preachers, for their own study, ought to look at the section of the discourse omitted (vv. 36-40), in part because it is important for what follows in vv. 41ff.

R. Bultmann (*John* [Philadelphia: Westminster, 1971], 221) brought greater clarity to the sequence by rearranging verses in the order 27, 34, 35, 30-33, 47-51a, 41-46, 36-40, a possibility that makes climactic what the lectionary omits! This sequence would explain v. 36, "I *said* to you that you have seen me and yet do not believe" (seeing is *not* believing; it depends on how you see). The Jews have seen Jesus, who (alone) has seen the Father, yet they do not believe in Jesus (v. 46; the best alternative reference for "I said" in v. 36 is v. 24, "you saw signs"). Verse 37, with its tone of predestination, will help explain v. 44. Verses 38-39 recount the purpose of Jesus' coming, to do God's will (cf. the Father's "seal" in v. 27) and to "lose nothing of all [neuter] that God has given me, but raise it up on the last day," phraseology helpful for interpreting 44b.

Verse 40 ties much together: The Father's will is "that everyone who sees the Son and believes in him [contrast v. 36; seeing can lead to believing, as with Thomas, John 20:29] may have eternal life; and I will raise that person up on the last day." Verse 40 might even be the preaching text for the whole pericope. "Eternal life" has been presented in 5:24 as the life of the age-to-come, now available in faith, and 5:28-29 added the aspect of fulfillment in a future resurrection.

The word for the complaining by the Jews in v. 41 is actually "murmur," a reminiscence of Israel in the wilderness, kicking and complaining about God's gifts (water, Exod. 15:24; manna, Exod. 16:2, 7, 12; cf. also Exod. 17:3; Num. 11:1; 14:2, 27). It became the legendary equivalent of disobedience (Ps. 106:25; 1 Cor. 10:10). Here they direct their complaint against Jesus on the grounds that they know his parents, so how could he have "come down from heaven"? Verse 42 is similar to the words in Mark 6:3, the rejection scene in Nazareth.

Jesus' response (43ff.) needs to be unpacked. Verse 44a sounds like predestination: no one can come to Jesus unless the Father "draws" him. The verb (also found at John 12:32) reflects Hos. 11:4 (God drew Israel with "bands of love") and Jer. 31:3 in the LXX ("I have drawn you into [my] mercy"). To such persons resurrection is promised. But this movement to Jesus and to faith by the Father's will (and, as Augustine said, God's grace; cf. John 1:12-13, 14d, 16) is not limited to an elect few but is potentially for all—all who will believe. This is made clear by use in v. 37 of "everything" (and "anyone" in NRSV) and in v. 45 by "all" and "everyone." "*Whoever* believes has eternal life" (v. 47, cf. the well-known "little gospel" of John 3:16, ". . . everyone who believes . . .").

But how does one come to faith as "the work of God" (6:29)? Here an unusual quotation from Isa. 54:13 plays a pivotal role in v. 45. One must be "taught by God." How so? By hearing Jesus (who alone has seen the Father, John 1:18) and thus learning from God. Jesus' remaining words in 6:47-51 hammer home the points that he, not Moses (Exod. 33:20-23), has seen God; that the Israelite ancestors who ate the manna gotten through Moses died, but Jesus offers bread, eaters of which will not die. Escalating each point, Jesus is the *living* bread (v. 51a); whoever eats of this bread will live *forever* (51b). The christological claim is clear, the benefits manifest, the means of appropriation obvious: by faith in Christ, eternal life.

There is considerable agreement that the bread-from-heaven discourse (6:32-51) is sapiential, that is, reflective of (OT) wisdom categories. Amos 8:11-12 provides a starting point with the threat from God of "a famine in the land; not . . . of bread, or a thirst for water, but of hearing the words of the Lord." Isaiah 55 depicts Yahweh inviting "everyone who thirsts" and those who spend money "for that which is not bread" to listen (= eat what is good) and live (55:1-3), for Yahweh's word is like rain on the land, providing "bread to the eater" and accomplishing the divine purpose (55:10-11). As is well known, Proverbs 8 and 9 depict Dame Wisdom inviting people to true life. This takes the form (9:5) of a banquet as the symbol of instruction and learning: "Come, eat of my bread and drink of the wine I have mixed." Sirach continues this picture, as Wisdom says, "Come to me . . . and eat your fill . . ." (24:18-21); she will feed "whoever fears the Lord" with "the bread of learning and give him the water of wisdom to drink" (cf. also Bar. 3:9—4:4). Ample background thus existed for depicting the partaking of wisdom as eating (bread) and drinking. Israel identified such wisdom with the Law (Moses). The NT regards Jesus Christ as wisdom (1 Cor. 1:30; it is a background for the Logos concept in John 1:1-4, 14). To term Jesus "bread from heaven" is a wisdom claim: he reveals the Father to everyone who responds in faith (cf. *TINT* 5.6; 7.4-10; 30.2).

Thus faith emerges as a main theme in this pericope (vv. 35, 37, 44, 45); it is the means of coming to God. Christology is another, in what Jesus claims in the "I am" statements (vv. 35, 41, 51). Is there anything eucharistic in these verses? Brown, who is sympathetic to the emphasis, allows it only as "secondary . . . undertones" and (AB 29:272–74) points out that there never was patristic agreement that it was eucharistic; even less among the reformers; and the Council of Trent "took no position" on the chapter (in part because the followers of John Huss appealed to v. 53 for communion in both kinds; cf. Schnackenburg, *John* 2:65–68). What of v. 51, at least the last clause? Jesus' statement about giving his flesh "for the life of the world" sounds to some like the formula in the last supper and Lord's Supper, "given for you." But the emphasis on eating as a symbol for learning of God is amply attested in wisdom imagery. For "give" see 4:14, and "flesh" in the Fourth Gospel is above all a reference to the incarnation (1:14) and Jesus' self-giving on the cross for the life of the world.

Next week's reading will get into the most patently eucharistic references in the Gospel of John. This week's Gospel reading calls for proclamation of Christ as the living bread and the possibility of faith for all who hear— and hence find life. They are "drawn" when they abandon their own judgment and "hear" and "learn" from God. The "drawing" is not *behind* but *in* the decision for faith, when one heeds the promise that no one who comes to Jesus will be cast out (6:37 RSV; Bultmann 231–32).

Thirteenth Sunday after Pentecost

Lutheran	Roman Catholic	Episcopal	Common Lectionary
Prov. 9:1-6	Prov. 9:1-6	Prov. 9:1-6	2 Sam. 18:24-33
Eph. 5:15-20	Eph. 5:15-20	Eph. 5:15-20	Eph. 5:15-20
John 6:51-58	John 6:51-58	John 6:53-59	John 6:51-58

FIRST LESSON: PROVERBS 9:1-6

This passage, where Wisdom invites those who are "simple" and "without sense" to her banquet, has great importance for understanding the bread discourse in John 6, as has already been indicated in the comments above on 6:24-35 and 41-51. Fuller (*Preaching*, 413) is among those who regret the failure of the *Ordo* to use the Proverbs passage earlier, given its great pertinence in the sapiential background to 6:32-51 (cf. R. Brown, AB 29:272–73).

The Common Lectionary's vivid account of how David learned of the death of his rebel son Absalom and his weeping lament in *2 Sam. 18:24-33* has been introduced in the notes on last week's OT readings. In exile at Mahanaim (17:27, across the Jordan, northeast of Jerusalem), David awaits word of the battle where his professional mercenaries defeated Absalom's larger force in the forest of Ephraim. The fleeing Absalom was caught by his head in oak branches (18:9; the Talmud adds that it was his much-prized hair [14:25-26] that trapped him). Joab, the realist, had him killed, and wanted a foreign Cushite to inform the king of the news. The swifter Ahimaaz enigmatically reports only the battle victory; either he tactfully omits Absalom's death (vv. 20, 28) or did not know of it (if the last part of v. 20 is the narrator's comment; cf. AB 9:408). David's "Would I had died instead" (v. 33) is something unsaid over Bathsheba's child (12:16-23). David's obsession here (19:4) compels Joab to call him back from a father's grieving to a king's duties (19:5-8).

How Prov. 9:1-6 fits into the development in the OT and Apocrypha of the theme of (eating) bread as participation in wisdom has been sketched in treating John 6:41-51. In a sermon, a reminder may be enough of how Proverbs 9 thus contributes to an understanding of reception by faith of God's wisdom and word as the way to life. The obvious link in today's Gospel is John 6:58b, "one who eats this bread will live forever." In 6:53-56 the application is blatantly eucharistic, though 6:63-64, 68-69 will offer a final "course correction" toward "word" and "faith."

If Prov. 9:1-6 is to be treated in its own right—and the figure of Lady Wisdom has obvious attractions for feminist theology—the picture ought to be developed not only in light of Proverbs 8 (Wisdom calls, 8:1; she who had a role in God's creation, 8:22-31) but also of 9:13-18. A female figure, Dame Folly, is employed also to personify the invitation to sensual pleasures, quick riches—and a doomed life (cf. 1:10-19; 7:1-27). The latter's invitation is to bed, the former's is to school, to learn (cf. 9:10-12). Some think the picture of "the foolish woman" is prior and that 9:1-6 is modeled on it (hence her "girls," 9:3), possibly with the "house" (9:1) a temple, involving cult and entry into righteousness (see Ezekiel 18 as teaching for such entry; W. McKane, *Proverbs* [OTL 1970], 360–65). But the house also suggests a school and even the whole creation (8:30-31), built upon "seven pillars" (9:1). The feast involves meat, bread, and wine (9:2, 5), that is, teachings that bring insight and life. The choice between the two ways, of life or of death (9:6, 18), is age-old and widespread. Jesus' hearers—and we—face such decisions, initially and frequently. Religion, in the sense of awe before God, reverence, and obedience, is "the beginning of wisdom" (9:10; 1:7).

SECOND LESSON: EPHESIANS 5:15-20

Ephesians 5:15-20 was read for centuries in lectionaries along with Matt. 22:1-14, the parable on the wedding feast. That pushed it in the direction of a sermon on how one lives "between the times" before the great marriage feast of the Lamb occurs. Its concatentation in *Ordo* lectionaries with John 6:51-58 threatens to move its worship references in 5:19-20 into an exclusively eucharistic direction (v. 20, *eucharistountes*), while the linkage with Prov. 9:1-6 about Lady Wisdom threatens to overstress its wisdom aspects in vv. 15b and 17 ("as wise," not foolish). Its concentration on the Spirit-filled community singing away by itself threatens to isolate church from the world in which its members live. (Attachment of v. 21 in older lectionaries and some translations like KJV and the Nestle Greek twenty-fifth edition—"submitting yourselves *to one another*"—heightens the isolation.) Verses 15-20 must be considered in their own context.

Most lectionaries bypass 5:3-14. The ethical parenesis there first frankly condemns sexual sins of various sorts (vv. 3-7). The contrast between the world of the Gentiles and Christians is then put in terms of darkness and light (vv. 8-14), age-old imagery (Gen. 1:2-5; Ps. 27:1; Isa. 9:2 = Matt. 4:13-16; 2 Cor. 4:6), sharpened in the Dead Sea Scrolls with language like that in 5:8 about community members as "children of light." The poetic lines in 5:14 likely quote a baptismal hymn: God awakens those dead in sins to life in Christ (2:1, 3-9, 12-13). The contrast between before and after the coming to faith ("once . . . now," v. 8) marks every Christian. To each of them and all together is addressed the imperative, "Keep on walking [living] as children of this Light" (v. 8).

The theme verse (15a) for 15-20 reiterates v. 8: Continue to look carefully (or precisely), therefore (in view of your attachment to Christ), at how you live (walk in ethical conduct). The following verses fall into three parts, each with a negative, then a positive assertion:

15b "not as unwise . . . but as wise" (*mē* . . . *alla* in Greek);
17 "not . . . foolish, but understand what the will of the Lord is" (i.e., the will of God known in Christ; cf. v. 10, "what is pleasing to the Lord");
18 "not . . . drunk with wine. . . , but be filled with the Spirit. . . ."

In elaborating each contrast, the author draws on Col. 3:16-17 and 4:5, the OT, and contemporary imagery. What Colossians had later (at 4:5), "Walk in wisdom toward them that are without, redeeming the time," has been put up front as the lead thought in 5:15-16. This "walk" (cf. 4:1, 17; 5:2), of those who are wise, concerns persons within the community (4:25, 32; contrast 5:7). The wisdom, from God (1:17), suggests discernment, to "redeem time" (*kairos*, opportune moment, not just *chronos*). The phrase is a commercial one, to "buy up time" in the sense of make the most of opportunities. The motivation is not, as so often in Paul, because the end is near but "because the days are evil," that is, the world and people around the Christian community (4:17-19; 5:3-8a; cf. 6:13). Hence the second admonition, emphasizing continuing discernment of the divine will. While unelaborated here, this will involves what has been revealed in God's plan and the gospel (1:8-14, 17-23; 3:2-6, 8-12, 18-19), via Scripture, Spirit, and church community.

The third admonition (5:18-20) may reflect three words of Prov. 23:31 in the LXX (Heb. and NRSV otherwise), but the warning to stop getting drunk applies wherever fermented beverages exist. There are no signs that a Dionysus cult or eucharistic orgies (cf. 1 Cor. 11:21-22; 2 Pet. 2:13) are involved. The contrast is with being continually filled with the Holy Spirit (1:13, cf. 1:17; 2:18, 22; 3:16; 4:3, 4, 30; 5:9; on divine "filling" and "fullness," cf. 3:19; 1:23; 4:10). No references follow to particular spiritual gifts or *charismata* given to each Christian (as in 1 Corinthians 12), but rather vv. 19-20 refer to communal expression of who they are in worship (cf. 1 Corinthians 14). This involves "speaking to one another" (v. 19a, RSV "addressing" each other; NRSV omits) and "singing and making melody to the Lord" (v. 19b), as well as "giving thanks" (v. 20, a general term, not in the NT a reference to celebrating Eucharist). No convincing distinctions among "psalms and hymns and spiritual songs" are apparent, though Christian compositions are likely meant (cf. 1 Cor. 14:26). The communal identity that emerges in giving thanks at all times and for all things is incipiently trinitarian: to the Father, in Christ's name, with the Spirit. Ostensibly, 5:15-20 is about conduct in the congregation, locally and universally. That a societal setting is not forgotten will become apparent in 5:20—6:20. Praise to God helps shape identity and sustain Christian life in the world. One emphasis here, as nowhere else in Ephesians, is on eschatology (which always influences ethics). Not the second coming but the first is formative for morality in this letter. Yet the very fact that Christians must be admonished about how they live shows that they are not yet permanently situated in the "heavenly realms" (1:3, 20; 2:6). They still struggle against the world in the world and against evil in heavenly places (6:12). They are people of two ages (1:21), who have Christ and the Spirit as pledge for their full and future inheritance (1:13-14).

GOSPEL: JOHN 6:51-59

Uncharacteristically, the lectionary begins with a rereading of last week's concluding verse, 6:51. That solves the debate over whether the verse goes with the previous section (so Schnackenburg, *John* 2:54–55, as a reference to Jesus' death) or with vv. 51-59 (Brown, AB 29:281, 291–92) or is to be divided (Bultmann, 234 holds that 6:51b, "and the bread . . . is my flesh," begins an editor's addition). This repetition also lifts up the claim of Jesus that "the Jews" in v. 52 dispute. The addition of v. 59 reiterates the location in Capernaum (6:17, 24); by adding "while Jesus was teaching in the synagogue," it also underscores the emphasis on teaching in the discourse (v. 45, "taught by God"; hearing and learning from the Father, by accepting Jesus' words; the synagogue here is a house of teaching, not worship).

The description of the Jews in v. 52 (they "disputed among themselves") is literally "fought" or "battled," possibly a reflection of Israel in the wilderness (Exod. 17:2, "the people quarreled with Moses"). This may be the place for the preacher to explain John's use of "the Jews" (a generic term, in place of "scribes, Pharisees," and so on, in the Synoptics). It will not do to substitute here "the leaders" or "Judeans" (as some paraphrases do out of philo-Semitic concerns), for we are in Capernaum of Galilee and the "crowd" of 6:2 and 6:24 is involved. John means by "the Jews" all who reject Jesus' claim. In his narrative about events of Jesus' day in Palestine and in light of the split between Jews and Christians in his day (cf. 16:2), the term was the natural one for the narrative, to present all who doubt or oppose the incarnate, crucified Christ. In this passage (6:53-54) it will include renegade Christians (see below).

What Jesus is reported to say in vv. 53-58 has been hotly debated as to origin and referent. Clearly there are many echoes of previous verses. The Jews' derogatory reference to Jesus in v. 52 as "this fellow" is the same Greek as in v. 42 (*houtos*). Jesus' initial response in v. 53 escalates the claim in vv. 35 and 51; "Son of Man" has been used in v. 27. The terms in v. 54 "eternal life" and "raise up on the last day" have appeared in v. 40. Even the seemingly new note in v. 56, "abide in me," has appeared in v. 27 (NRSV, "food that endures for eternal life"). "The Father" (v. 57) has been spoken of in vv. 32, 44, 46. The contrast in v. 58 to the bread (manna) which "your ancestors ate"—and died, is found verbatim in v. 49. Such links can be taken as signs of continuity from the same author or of an able redactor who wishes to give the whole discourse a new twist, that is, a distinct reference to the Lord's Supper.

The options sketched above from Léon-Dufour for the chapter (see Pentecost 11 on 6:24-35) are spelled out by Schnackenburg (*John* 2:58–59) with reference to vv. 52-58; each has good commentators behind it (we shall cite mostly Roman Catholics as examples; references in Schnackenburg): (*a*) the evangelist planned vv. 52-58, the eucharistic section, as a continuation and application of the metaphysical or sapiential vv. 31-51 (H. Schürmann); (*b*) two audiences are in the evangelist's mind—unbelieving Jews and Christians with a false sacramentology (Gnostics or Docetists who, in 1 John, reject Christ-in-the-flesh; H. Leroy); (*c*) a later hand added vv. 51-59, but from within the Johannine school, using earlier Lord's Supper traditions (R. Brown); (*d*) vv. 51b-58 is a later addition to make the Fourth Gospel overtly sacramental (Bultmann) or to correct a misunderstanding by some Christians about the book (G. Richter). It is at this point that every interpreter and preacher must make a choice—often all too readily guided by denominational or personal views on the Eucharist. But in which direction?

Léon-Dufour (*Sharing* 258–60) has shown how even vv. 52-58 can be read in a sapiential way. To eat and drink as described here is an extremely vivid way of talking in wisdom language about receiving Jesus in faith, interiorization of the covenant in an abiding way. Many others use the Lord's Supper itself (as they understand it) as the hermeneutical solution to "eucharisticize" the entire chapter (cf. *Proclamation 2* on this passage, p. 29, although the exegete [p. 26] feels "the evangelist wished to defamiliarize his readers with the traditional understanding of the Lord's Supper").

Confessional traditions handle the material with care; for instance, the Lutheran *Book of Concord* concludes for reception of Christ spiritually, by faith, yet also "orally" (in the mouth), but not in a "Capernaitic" fashion, but a "supernatural" and "heavenly" manner. Recent guitar ditties press people to "eat his body, drink his blood," without hinting how cannibalistic and repugnant to the OT outlook that would be (Gen. 9:4; Lev. 3:17; Deut. 12:23). What is really repugnant to the Jews, however, is that this is *Jesus'* flesh and blood, his person in an abiding relationship. No wonder Brown (AB 29:cxi–cxiv, 300) takes a mediating view on Johannine sacramentology, while stressing Eucharist, though there is more to come in next week's reading. Finally the preacher must contend with the fact that the *Ordo* chose Prov. 9:1-6 (the sapiential background!) for the reading this week, though it was pertinent for Pentecost 12 as well. Does that complement eucharistic emphases in 6:51-58?

It is obvious that this week's Gospel reading emphatically repeats the claim of Jesus to be the true life-giving bread (6:53, 54, 55, 56, 57), whom the individual must receive in order to have Life. The assertion is now made in bald, offensive terms ("gnaw flesh, drink blood"). The passage, against "the Jews" and Christians who reject a Jesus come-in-the-flesh (1 John 4:1-2), has narrowed the issue, seemingly, to the Eucharist (6:53, no life unless you eat and drink . . .). That blurs what has been the offense in the rest of chap. 6 and the whole Gospel of John: Jesus himself is the revealer of God; what he teaches is about himself ("I am . . . "), and, when received in faith, means Life of the new age. Receiving the sacrament can express this focus but may run the danger of mechanical oversimplification of faith and discipleship. The Eucharist points to Christ, incarnate and crucified, and to an abiding relationship by faith to Christ as the one who reveals God. It is the Word and his words (8:31, 38, 43, 51; 14:24) that are vital, as the next reading will make clear.

The structure of the Three-Year Lectionary has led to a tendency to preach on the Gospel for the day, a move abetted by the liturgical custom of having it read by the preacher just before the sermon. An obvious criticism is that the OT choices are not encouraged to speak in their own right as Scripture. Epistle readings have often been ignored in proclamation, a tendency strengthened by current emphasis on narrative, to the loss of propositional thinking, acclamations, and ethical admonition. The hermeneutic in this Proclamation *volume follows that of the lectionary, sometimes corrected by the Scriptures themselves read historically. Local applications, outlines, and anecdotes are the tasks of the preacher, under the text.*

Fourteenth Sunday after Pentecost

Lutheran	Roman Catholic	Episcopal	Common Lectionary
Josh. 24:1-2a, 14-18	Josh. 24:1-2a, 15-17, 18b	Josh. 24:1-2a, 14-25	2 Sam. 23:1-7
Eph. 5:21-31	Eph. 5:21-32	Eph. 5:21-33	Eph. 5:21-33
John 6:60-69	John 6:60-69	John 6:60-69	John 6:55-69

FIRST LESSON: JOSHUA 24:1-2a, 14-25

The pledge of the people to serve the Lord during a covenant-making assembly at Shechem in Joshua 24 is the highlight of this OT reading in RC, L, and E lectionaries (give or take a few verses difference). The obvious parallels with the Gospel for the day, where Jesus' disciples are confronted with the claims for him in the bread-of-life discourse (John 6:60-69), lie in the need for decision: to go with him or turn away. Peter's confession (6:68-69) is the counterpart to "we will serve the Lord" (Josh. 24:15, 18). Dramatic challenge ("choose this day," Josh. 24:15; "do you also wish to go away?" John 6:67) and confessional commitment are thus points in common.

For those following the David cycle in CL, these "last words" of the son of Jesse in *2 Sam. 23:1-7* may seem anticlimactic and even arrogant to some, when his whole career is considered. The tendency to assign a late dating to the passage has now given way to some support for an early date, even one in David's day, in part because v. 1 is reminiscent of Balaam's oracles (Num. 24:3, 15). The Hebrew for "sweet psalmist of Israel" (KJV; cf. 2 Samuel 22) may also be taken to refer to his anointed status as Yahweh's favorite (NRSV). In vv. 2-4 David speaks as a prophet of how a just king is to rule. Verse 5a claims God's endorsement of David's house, on the basis of an "everlasting" or unconditional covenant (5b; cf. 2 Sam. 7:14; Ps. 89:28-37). The fate of the godless stands in contrast (23:6-7). But was David's reign always so just and blessed? Compare 2 Samuel 20–21. His house did not continue forever as a dynasty. The lines are thus more pro-David than biblical history allows. Yet vv. 3b-4 provide an ideal for future kings—and for all of us.

In the lectionary's excerpts from the last chapter of Joshua, the people of Israel are gathered at Shechem (24:1-2a), a city and cult site (Mounts Ebal and Gerazim, Deuteronomy 27; Josh. 8:30-35) north of Jerusalem. Joshua confronts them in vv. 14-15 with the demand to serve the Lord and put away other lords; he ends with his own witness to the choice for Yahweh by himself and his household. (By omitting v. 14 and "in Egypt," the *Ordo* poses a choice between pagan gods of Mesopotamia and pagan gods where they now dwell. Joshua's own decision then stands out all the more.) The choice of the people, to serve Yahweh, is couched in a description of the Lord (vv. 17-18) that is characteristic of salvation history and cult declarations. It echoes the recital of Yahweh's victories in vv. 2b-13, which the lectionary leaves out, a story cast in the first person ("I brought you out" of Egypt), concentrating on Abraham, the exodus (vv. 5-7, 17a), and the conquest (vv. 8-13, 17b-18). (The *Ordo* fastidiously skips over the driving out of the Amorites, in v. 18a.) Sinai and the covenant and law are unmentioned.

The RC and L versions close with the confession of, and pledge to serve, the Lord. L and E, by including v. 14, offer two excellent points in the phrase "serve . . . in sincerity" and "in faithfulness"—totally and with trustworthiness. By adding vv. 19-25 the E reading interposes the warning that, because Yahweh is a holy and jealous/zealous God, the people cannot "serve God" as easily as they suppose. Their commitment is probed and then reaffirmed (vv. 20-24). Thus Joshua made a covenant. Some see here reflection of how people in the Shechem area, who had not been conquered by the sword, entered into Israel via a covenant. Others see reflected a later periodic "covenant renewal" ceremony (cf. Deut. 11:26-28) and an ancient credo used in cult (24:2-13; cf. Deut. 6:21-23; 26:5-9). It is a story about Joshua's day, retold by the Deuteronomist for his day four centuries later. The lectionary uses the passage to pose questions of decision and commitment during the ministry of Jesus and for the Johannine community—as well as for us. Usually the language of choice and election is employed for God choosing us; here, for our reponse (cf. 24:3ff., "I took," "I gave," and 15, "choose"; and John 6:65, 69).

SECOND LESSON: EPHESIANS 5:21-33

This complex passage challenges the preacher or teacher to deal with marriage, ecclesiology, or both. Marriage is the likely emphasis if one ends with v. 31, as in the L reading, or with v. 33 (E and CL); ecclesiology and possibly sacraments are more likely if one ends with v. 32 (*Ordo*). The primary structure of 5:22—6:10 is that of a "table of household duties" (*Haustafeln*), traditionally involving subordinate persons (wives, 5:22; children, 6:1; slaves, 6:5) in relation to superiors (husbands, 5:25; fathers, 6:4; masters, 6:9). This material draws on Col. 3:18—4:1 (cf. 1 Pet. 2:13—3:7). Pentecost 14 is the only occasion when *Ordo*-style lectionaries assign such material, and then only the husband-wife part (perhaps with an ecclesial interest; cf. also *Ordo*, Holy Family, Year A, Col. 3:12-21). Into 5:22-33 has been inserted extensive material on Christ and the church (vv. 23b-24a, 25b-27, 29b-30, 32b). Marriage and ecclesiology are riveted together by use of the phrase "(just) as [Greek *hōs* or *kathōs*] Christ . . ." (vv. 23, 25, 29; cf. also 24, 28), as well as by the enigmatic v. 32, "This [marriage? Christ and the church?] is a great mystery."

Dare one preach today on what many hear as a patriarchal view of marriage? If the passage is read in the liturgy, dare one fail to explain it? Opinions on it vary, including Markus Barth's contention that Paul here was opposing an excessive feminist revolution of total emancipation in his day (AB 34A:655–62) and is setting forth a Christian view of marriage as a covenant based solely on Christ (738–53). Recent research has helped make clear that the *Haustafel* form stemmed from the Greek view of household (and civic) management found in Aristotle and other philosophers. Deeply embedded in the Greco-Roman world, this subordination structure was taken over by Hellenistic Judaism and Christianity after Paul, as part of the coming to terms with the social order of the day (*VU* 109–10, 115; Lincoln, WBC 42:355–65). But the subordinationalist structure is here modified, if not ultimately dismantled, by placing v. 20 over the whole, as well as by limiting subordination to marriage (in contrast to all women with regard to all men) and by qualifying the relationship through emphasis on love, self-sacrifice, and Christ's lordship.

The key to all relationships, in marriage and in the church, is expressed in v. 21 as *mutual* subjection. This injunction is addressed to the whole congregation, "superiors" included. Both church leaders and husbands are forced to rethink and revise the positions in which "creation" and social structures, even if seemingly divinely sanctioned here, have placed them. NRSV nicely arranges v. 21 as a separate paragraph. This indicates its summary character for community and worship (5:15-20, for it attaches grammatically to "be filled with the Spirit," as a fifth participle—speaking, singing, making melody, giving thanks, being subject), and also indicates how it stands over and trumps what is said on wives/husbands, children/ fathers, slaves/masters (5:22—6:9). The passage on marriage is further bracketed by two references to fear (*phobos*) in vv. 21 and 33, which (N)RSV makes more palatable for moderns by blunting the force as "reverence" and "respect" (but cf. OT "fear of the Lord" and the biblical sense of proper but not slavish awe).

The preacher who expounds these verses on marriage ought to wrestle with "headship" (v. 23, authority, expressed in self-giving love); the stress on *agapē* (Barth, AB 34A:701 n. 360 quotes the line from *Camelot* on "how to handle a woman": "Love her, *love* her, love *her*"); the reflection of Lev. 19:18 at 5:33 ("*love your* wife *as yourself*"); the sexual eros component in marriage (v. 31, "one *flesh*"); and marriage as companionship ("covenant" is not used in Ephesians, but cf. Mal. 2:14) (Barth, 704–8, 715–29, 749–53). What of ecclesiology? The universal church is viewed in light of Christ as head of the body and savior (v. 23), who gave himself for her (v. 25; cf. 1:22-23; 4:15-16; 5:2b). Verses 25b-27, which may reflect a hymnic tradition, employ a variety of images (cf. Ezek. 16:8-14; 2 Cor. 11:2, marriage customs, including the bridal bath; baptism) to stress the role of the word (*rhēma*, 6:17; Rom. 10:8, 17) in creating a resplendently pure community for Christ. Christ cares for and nourishes us, "members of his body" (vv. 29-30). Some see in v. 29 a reference to the Lord's Supper, along with baptism in v. 26; the infamous Vulgate rendering of *mystērion* in v. 32 as *sacramentum* has led to views of marriage as a sacrament in a later sense—plainly a position beyond what Ephesians says (EKK 256, 258; AB 34A:744–49). The "nurture" language is better seen as family imagery (6:4; 1 Thess. 2:7) such as occurred in marriage contracts in the papyri (WBC 42:379–80). Christ's word (v. 26) takes many forms in church life, and the author clearly says the mystery here (cf. 6:19; 1:9; 3:3-5, 9) is the gospel news about Christ and the church. Overall, one social institution, Christ's church—in Ephesians, part of God's plan for salvation (3:9-11)—interplays with another, marriage, for those in Christ.

GOSPEL: JOHN 6:60-69

The discourse on Jesus as the bread of life in 6:31-51, read on Pentecost 11 and 12, emphasized Christology (Jesus is the one who has come down from heaven, whom people hear and so learn from the Father) and faith (as the response that, in appropriating Jesus, leads to eternal life). Verses 53-58 added an insistence on appropriating the Son of Man through eating and drinking, a symbol not only for receiving Wisdom's teaching but also for a mutual abiding of disciples and Christ through the Lord's Supper. Increasingly there has been emphasis on "flesh," which Jesus gives for the life of the world (vv. 51b, 53-55), a reference to his incarnation and crucifixion.

The reactions of the listeners to these bold statements conclude the chapter in vv. 60-69. (The lectionary omits vv. 70-71, on the "devil" member of the chosen twelve, Judas Iscariot, who "was going to betray" Jesus; vv. 70-71 make specific the identity of the traitor mentioned in v. 64 and thus provide another pointer to the cross; cf. 12:4; 13:26-27; 18:2-5). These reactions fall into two parts: defection by many (vv. 60-66) and confession by some (vv. 67-69). Most surprising is that neither "the crowd" nor "the Jews" are mentioned. Instead, Jesus' *disciples* are involved. Jesus pushes them to decision. The result, as Bultmann puts it (*John*, 443), is separation, indeed within the disciple circle itself. It is dangerous for lukewarm followers to hear Jesus' real claims.

The first of two narrative dialogues (vv. 60-66) begins with some of his disciple-hearers exclaiming about how fantastic and offensive Jesus' teaching is. The reference is not just to eucharistic teaching (if vv. 53-58 are so interpreted) but to the entire discourse about who Jesus is and what he effects (vv. 35-58). Kierkegaard once took "this *logos*" in v. 60 (NRSV, "this teaching") as a reference to the Word of John 1:1-18, Jesus himself. Ultimately, that is correct, but it is the "I am" claim in the teaching that will cause the parting of the ways. Those who "complain" (murmur, v. 61; same verb used of "the Jews" in v. 41) are disciples. Jesus "knows this in himself" (RSV is more literal); as with v. 64, supernatural knowledge is implied (as at 2:23-25). He takes the lead; if there is offense in this claim (about his being the bread that comes down from heaven), he asks, what if the Son of Man were to ascend where he was before, in other words, to the Father? (cf. 6:27; 1:51). This will involve, in the Fourth Gospel, the Son of Man's being lifted up (on a cross) before glorification (8:28; 3:13-15; 17:5). Then he will be able to give them eternal life (6:27). Jesus' uncompleted question to the disciples may seek to arouse faith, but the conclusion can also be, "Then you really will be scandalized."

Verse 63a is much debated. Some print "spirit" (in contrast to "flesh") with lower-case *s* (RSV, NEB, NRSV), but others capitalize it as a reference to the Holy Spirit (KJV, CEV, R. Brown). It can be applied to Jesus: not in his fleshly existence but only as ascended Son of Man, can he bestow the life-giving Spirit (7:39). Or it could apply to the believer, as "flesh" incapable, as Spirit-born able to enter the kingdom (cf. 3:6-13).

The matter is complicated further by debate over whether "flesh" here has anything to do with Jesus' "flesh" eaten to bring life in vv. 51b-57. Absolutely not, says Brown (AB 29:299, 303). In *Proclamation* (1975, pp. 25–26) R. H. Hiers sees the verse apparently repudiating the "materialistic" understanding in vv. 51-57; similarly A. Y. Collins in *Proclamation 2* (1982, p. 32) questions a literal understanding of eating flesh; it is "the *teaching* of Jesus" that "gives eternal life."

Verse 63b is some help in this matter. That Jesus' words are spirit (Spirit) and life certainly supports the latter view, but if his words include those in vv. 51-58, then the teaching also involves the Eucharist. The most likely explanation is that originally vv. 60-61 referred to the discourse in vv. 31-51. Jesus' claim, accepted in faith, brings life; the disciple's flesh is useless, God's Spirit is needed. Once vv. 51b-58 are factored in, the matter becomes more complicated. "Flesh," as the person born of flesh, is useless, but to be born of the Spirit gives life. However, Jesus' flesh in the incarnation and in the self-giving on the cross is not subject to this stricture.

In the total, redacted chapter, simply put, v. 63 advances the argument another step: beyond all emphasis on the Eucharist is the Spirit—and the words of Jesus. Or better, the Spirit and Jesus' words give the Lord's Supper its significance. In any case, some disciples do not believe the unfolding teaching (v. 64). This Jesus knows, and the principle of the Father's granting (drawing) individuals to Jesus is reasserted (v. 65; cf. vv. 37, 44).

Why "disciples" in this passage, many of whom stop following Jesus when confronted with his claim and pressed for faith? As elsewhere (cf. 8:30-40, 59), John is showing how, when push comes to shove, followers can desert Jesus. The passage here moves from the crowd and the Jews to disciples as examples of people offended at Jesus' word. Here the evangelist is speaking of and to Christians of a sort in his own day. They are persons who reject the claims made for Jesus in the Johannine Gospel and community. Proclamation of Christ always leads to crisis and decision. Some decided he is not the bread of life (6:60, 64, 66) or incarnate Son of God and ultimately left the community (1 John 4:1b-3; 2:19; 5:13). That could happen in Jesus' day, John's, or ours.

All the more important, then, is the positive example of faithful confession of Jesus (6:67-69). Peter speaks for the Twelve, in a counterpart to the Caesarea Philippi scene in Matthew 16 (cf. Mark 8, below, Pentecost 17). Who else is there like Jesus? Note v. 68b, "You have the words of eternal life." Jesus' words bring life. To "come to believe and know" (v. 69) implies one action, of faith and understanding; faith does have a noetic aspect, often overlooked nowadays. Here, that aspect means Jesus as "the Holy One of God," a little used title (but cf. Mark 1:24). In John, the Father is holy (17:11), who has made holy and sent into the world his Son (10:36); Jesus is thus the revelation of God. Many reject this; some confess it. Proclamation is to make clear the claim and the offense, as well as Jesus' promise of life when, to the one who says, "I am the bread of life," we say, "You are the revelation of the Holy God."

Fifteenth Sunday after Pentecost

Lutheran	Roman Catholic	Episcopal	Common Lectionary
Deut. 4:1-2, 6-8	Deut. 4:1-2, 6-8	Deut. 4:1-9	1 Kings 2:1-4, 10-12
Eph. 6:10-20	James 1:17-18, 21 b-22, 27	Eph. 6:10-20	Eph. 6:10-20
Mark 7:1-8, 14-15, 21-23	Mark 7:1-8, 14-15, 21-23	Mark 7:1-8, 14-15, 21-23	Mark 7:1-8, 14-15, 21-23

FIRST LESSON: DEUTERONOMY 4:1-9

As the Gospel readings return to Mark after five weeks in John 6, an OT lesson is chosen in most "first generation" *Ordo* lectionaries to match Mark 7; specifically the emphasis Jesus puts on "the commandment of God" (Mark 7:8, cf. 7:9) in contrast to "human precepts," that is, "the traditions of the [Jewish] elders" (7:7 and 7:3). The words of Moses in the concluding part of the prologue (Deuteronomy 1–4) of his "farewell address" to Israel—for that is what this second presentation of the Torah amounts to, set forth for the Deuteronomists' day in the seventh century B.C.—lift up "the commandments of the Lord your God" (4:2). They are to be obeyed, and neither added to nor subtracted from, as the later interpretative tradition did, according to Jesus' critique.

The CL (*2 Kings 2:1-4, 10-12*) concludes its fifteen weeks of David's story with a scene of the king (whose "last words" were read last week according to 2 Samuel 23) handing over his throne and some advice to his successor, Solomon. Appropriately, 1 Kings 2:10-12 is a summary of David's forty-year reign, with burial of the seventy-year-old monarch in Jerusalem on the slope of Ophal. Verses 1 and 10 frame the "farewell speech," where, as in Joshua 23, typical Deuteronomistic themes appear in vv. 2-4, especially that obedience to God's commandments brings a blessing. If Solomon and others live thus, the dynasty will continue (2:3). They, of course, did not. Although the Davidic dynasty continued for almost four centuries, it was full of more "downs" than "ups." The lectionary glosses over the final tragic years of David's reign and omits the advice in 2:5-9 about how to handle three figures from David's past: for two of the three, kill them! The case of Joab (whose murder is carried out in 2:28-34) is the most familiar, going back to the murder of Absalom (2 Sam.

18:5, 10, 14). Thus David remains, like most of us, a mixture of high-minded faithfulness and pragmatic ruthlessness. Blessing and curse go on. In appointing only vv. 1-2 and 6-8 of Deuteronomy 4, the RC and L readings mean to focus on five points: (*a*) obedience ("give heed," "observe," "keep") diligently to (*b*) God's law (v. 8, "statutes and ordinances," 4:1, *ḥōq, mišpạt,* positive decrees and decisions in "case law"), with (*c*) a blessing (the land God gives). God is the basis or indicative for the imperatives (vv. 7-8; cf. 4:32-40). While the admonition not to "add" or "take away" anything is characteristic of ancient law codes (v. 2; Code of Hammurabi, treaty of Esarhaddon), it also points to (*d*) "canonical status" of what God commands (cf. Rev. 22:18-19). It "fixes" the text. It may (but need not) exclude adaptability to later situations. (*e*) Lives conformed to the "word" (v. 2, RSV, *dābār*) of God point to God's "nearness" (cf. Deut. 30:11-14) through that teaching, which is Israel's counterpart to "wisdom" among other peoples (vv. 6-7).

If the passage is dealt with in its own right, it is well to situate the emphasis on doing the entire Torah of God in the context of Deuteronomy 1–3. These chapters, especially 1:6—3:11, are a historical recital of how God led Israel from Sinai (Horeb) to the promised land, parts of which, east of the Jordan River, are already being allotted among the tribes (3:12-17). The covenant structure includes what God has done to deliver the people and also what God has said to guide them. But it is Joshua, not Moses, who will lead them on in the "Holy War" (3:18-29). The E lectionary calls for vv. 3-5, including how God punished sexual misadventures and idolatry at Peor (Num. 25:1-9), as a spur to obedience. Verse 9 adds the necessity of transmitting the narrative and teaching to coming generations. Interpreters should be careful not to read a Law/Gospel or OT/NT dichotomy into the lectionary's use of Deuteronomy 4 and Mark. Jesus will affirm the commandments (specifically Deut. 5:16 at Mark 7:9); the contrast is with "human additions."

SECOND LESSON: EPHESIANS 6:10-20

The long-established practice of pairing Eph. 6:10-17 (or 10-20), about the *militia Christi* battling Satan, with a miracle story about Jesus battling evil (John 4:46b-53) or in controversy (Matt. 22:15-21), has been lost in the *Ordo*, which relegates 6:10-20 to a weekday reading in order to get in more from James on Sundays (see Pentecost 16 below). Yet 6:10-20 confronts one with a cosmic conflict that is part of the situation of church and believers and with a renewed call for prayer and gospel proclamation.

For Ephesians 6, Colossians provided a partial model through its words at 4:2-4 about prayer and the apostle's revealing of the word. Ephesians, with its detailed picture of battle panoply for the saints, draws on a long OT tradition of God as divine warrior (Exod. 15:3; Isa. 42:13; Ps. 7:12-13) and the Holy War theme (Exod. 14:13-14; Josh. 10:7-11; Ps. 35:1-8; Hab. 3:8-9; Wis. 5:17-23). The most influential passage is Isa. 59:15b-17, about Yahweh buckling on armor to avenge justice and truth, along with Isa. 11:5 on how the anointed king is clothed with righteousness and faithfulness. Some feel the imagery in Eph. 6:11-17 is too abrupt in a document emphasizing peace (2:14-15, 17; 4:3), but the paradox fits with other assertions about a world alienated from God (2:1-3, 12; 4:18-19, 27), where Satan attacks. Note vv. 12, 13, "this present darkness," "that evil day." Rhetorical criticism sees in this *peroratio* reflections of chapter 1 (compare 6:10 with 1:19), but the closing section does far more than repeat earlier ideas. There is a link with the household relationships described in 5:21—6:9: the cosmos as the scene for struggle in 6:12 is the household (and state) writ large.

Verses 11-13 set forth the basic contrast: in a universe where God the creator (3:15) reigns and Christ has won the costly victory (5:2b), rebel powers of evil, led by the devil (cf. also 2:2; 4:27), still threaten. So take up God's armor (vv. 14-17)! Older commentators suggested that Paul wrote this description of a soldier's equipment while chained to a Roman guard (cf. 6:20 "in chains"), but the background is even broader, in the OT Holy War, creation myths, world-religions speculations, Greek philosophy, and the "War Scroll" from Qumran (Barth, AB 34A:787–93). Seneca spoke of life as a battle (*vivare militare est, Ep.* 96.5). The items here can be analyzed through the verbs ("take up," v. 13; "stand," v. 14; "put on," v. 15; "take," vv. 16, 17; perhaps from a Christian catechism) or the OT references to God's armor now given to Christians, or the metaphors about truth, righteousness (justification), and faith(fulness of God). The sword comes from the Spirit and is the word of God (4:26).

Somewhat surprisingly, the final paragraph (vv. 18-20) stresses prayer. A series of terms for prayer are make the point, not that we have here a seventh weapon, but that prayer always goes with the word and God's armor. That people are asked to pray for Paul in prison echoes Col. 4:4, but also strikes a further note: the word must be declared with boldness, in whatever circumstances. When God speaks and arms us, we must speak (2 Cor. 4:13). Thus the gospel advances. To Christians, threatened and in conflict, Eph. 6:10-20 has often spoken heroically, from Ignatius of Antioch ("Let your baptism be your arms, faith your helmet, love your spear, endurance your armor," *Polycarp* 6.2) to Ignatius Loyola; to people as different as the humanist Erasmus ("A Handbook for the Christian Soldier") or Heinrich Vogel's "Iron Rations of the Christian" in the Hitler period, Sabine Baring Gould's "Onward, Christian Soldiers," and most reformers against corruption and for liberation (cf. Schnackenburg, EKK, 337–42, "Spiritual Military Service").

GOSPEL: MARK 7:1-8, 14-15, 21-23

These excerpts, from the longest unit of teaching by Jesus in Mark since 4:1-34, set forth the theme of "clean/unclean" (NRSV "defiled," 7:2, 15, 18, 20, 23) in law and life. The pericope returns to Mark after five weeks of readings from John 6. On Pentecost 9, Mark 6:30-34 told how the Twelve had returned from their preaching mission and Jesus "began to teach" the crowd (6:34). Then followed the feeding of the five thousand (6:35-44), the storm at sea where Jesus walked on the water (6:47-52), and arrival at Gennesaret (on the northwest side of the Lake of Galilee), where crowds again gathered (6:53-56). Two readings in Mark 7, this Sunday and next, resume sequential sections through chapter 13, another discourse (on the last things).

On Mark's Gospel, written around A.D. 70, see D. J. Harrington, *NJBC* #41; *VU* 49–53; P. J. Achtemeier, *ABD* 4:541–57; *TINT* 121–28 (#25). Morna Hooker, *Mark* (Black's NT Commentary [London 1991], 1–5) shows the changed interests of commentators over the last forty years, from "what happened" historically to source, form, and redaction in tradition history, and from Jesus' or Mark's meaning to that chosen by readers today. For her, Mark is a pastor-theologian. Some characteristics of Mark appear in 7:1-23: It is written for gentile Christians (hence the parenthetical explanations in 7:3-4 and 11, and use of the LXX at vv. 6-7 and 10) and employs a list of vices (21b-22), such as was common in Hellenistic Judaism and Paul (Col. 3:5-8; cf. Eph. 5:3-5).

Mark 7:1 begins with exactly the same words in Greek as 6:30; this time it is "Pharisees and some of the scribes" from Jerusalem, not disciples, who gather around Jesus. The conversation will be with opponents, not pupils. These Jerusalem opponents are also a pointer to the passion (cf. 3:22; 10:33). A controversy ensues when they see Jesus' disciples eat with "defiled" hands. This is explained as unwashed hands and then with a further laundry list (vv. 3-4) of items that "all the Jews" wash. Hygiene is not the issue but ritual, observance of "the tradition of the elders." One Mishnah tractate deals with "Hands" (6.11 *Yadaim*), but not everything in vv. 3-4 can be documented for Jesus' day, let alone as practice for "all Jews"; it is a generalization about priestly injunctions that were adopted by (some) Pharisees and Essenes. NRSV omits an uncertain word that may mean "wash 'with a handful' of water" or "with the fist." The Pharisees criticize Jesus' disciples, but Jesus defends them (vv. 2, 5-8), as in 2:23-28. The quotation shifts the issue from unclean hands to lips and hearts, but the consistent target is human tradition in contrast to God's command (vv. 3, 7, 8).

The lectionary skips vv. 9-13 about the device of "Corban" ("dedicated to God," so not for other uses). It picks up in vv. 14-15 the shift in audience (the crowd, cf. 6:45) but misses the disciples (v. 17) as addressees for vv. 21-23. The most important saying in 7:1-23 is v. 15: Jesus contrasts what enters from the outside (undefiling) with what comes out of a person (corrupting). This can be (and is in v. 19) explained as a reference to food eaten and excreted into the privy. The comment in v. 19b is the most revealing in the chapter on Jewish kosher food laws: Jesus thus "declared all foods clean" (cf. 1 Cor. 10:25-27, 31). This is the eventual position of Paul and the Hellenistic church. But if Jesus spoke so clearly, why was there debate about what Christians were free to eat? (Cf. 1 Cor. 8:7-13; Rom. 14:2-6; Acts 15:19-20, 29.) Because 7:15 is somewhat ambiguous, it could also refer to words and thoughts. Indeed, that is how, on repetition in v. 20, it is understood in vv. 21-23: Evil inclinations from within defile a person. The list of corrupting vices consists of six in the plural (in the Greek) and six in the singular (KJV is more literal here; "an evil eye" = NRSV "envy"; cf. Prov. 28:22 KJV; Sir. 14:9-10; Deut. 15:9, begrudging, hostility). Sex, violence, and ego are prominent in these "moral boomerangs" from within. The application to eating foods arises from the context of 7:2-4a, 5, and 19.

The interpreter would do well to start with v. 15 and develop the saying's meanings in terms of (a) thoughts, words, actions (vv. 20-23, 6b) and (b) foods (vv. 1-5, 19). Ultimately it is a matter of human injunctions versus God's command (vv. 6b-8, 9-13, 19b). Jesus interpreted the saying by the way he aided even Gentiles (7:24-30, 31-37), broke legal barriers (1:41; 5:41, touching a corpse; 5:27-28), and ate with sinners (2:15-17). The disciples had trouble understanding (7:18) the freedom of Jesus. For disciples today the preacher can give attention to (1) how evil comes from within us ("the heart") and (2) attitude toward traditions and to the law. The tendency, when Deuteronomy 4 is also read, is to tone down the liberating sense in the Gospel text.

Sixteenth Sunday after Pentecost

Lutheran	Roman Catholic	Episcopal	Common Lectionary
Isa. 35:4-7a	Isa. 35:4-7a	Isa. 35:4-7a	Prov. 2:1-8
James 1:17-22, 26-27	James 2:1-5	James 1:17-27	James 1:17-27
Mark 7:31-37	Mark 7:31-37	Mark 7:31-37	Mark 7:31-37

FIRST LESSON: ISAIAH 35:4-7a

The choice of these verses is obvious. The prophetic reference to how, in the restoration of the exiles from Babylon to Zion, "the ears of the deaf" will be "unstopped" and "the tongue of the speechless sing for joy" (vv. 5b, 6b) finds fulfillment in Jesus' healing of a deaf man with an impediment in his speech (Mark 7:32, 35). Mark does not use explicit OT quotations with an introductory formula, as Matthew does ("This happened in order that it might be fulfilled which was spoken by the prophet, saying . . ."), and this Markan miracle story is not recounted in Matthew or Luke. But the description in Mark 7:32 of the person as having "an impediment in his speech" (Greek *mogilalon*, "speaking with difficulty"; contrast 7:35, "speaking plainly") seems to reflect the same Greek word found in Isa. 35:6 LXX (NRSV "the speechless" person). Mark (or a source) must have had this passage in mind, one that was elsewhere also applied to Jesus' deeds (Matt. 11:5, par. Luke 7:22; cf. Isa. 35:5-6; in the lectionary, Advent 3, Year A).

The choice of *Prov.* 2:1-8 in CL, after the long David saga, is more difficult to explain. The next four weeks in CL will feature wisdom literature (Proverbs and Job). These verses urge a pupil to heed words of wisdom and so attain knowledge of God. Attentiveness and searching are required. Are the verses meant to direct one to the epistle that follows from the NT "wisdom book" of James? God as a shield (vv. 7b, 8b) and "paths of justice" (8a) are attractive emphases for a "way of life."

Isaiah 35 is the glowing counterpart to grim chapter 34 and its picture of the destruction of God's enemies, especially Edom, an age-old opponent (Num. 24:18; Isa. 11:14; Amos 1:11-12; Jer. 49:7-22). With Edom smitten (Isa. 34:5, 6, 9, "No Kingdom There," v. 12), the exiles will be able to make their way in safety back to Zion from the Babylonian exile, with no fear of passing through hostile lands. The reading does not include 35:1-2 about how the wilderness (the rift of the Jordan) will blossom with

God's glory, nor the picture of a *sacra via*, a Holy Way for God's people (v. 8), or even reference to Zion (Jerusalem) as the goal (v. 10). But it does echo God's vengeance (on Edom, not Israel, v. 4d) and the old admonitions needed to encourage pilgrims to undertake the journey (vv. 3-4). The apocalyptic detail in v. 9, as in the "peaceable kingdom" (cf. 11:6-9), is not read, but the restoration of dry places through water in the desert is (vv. 6b-7).

The entire passage has affinity with Isaiah 40–55, especially in v. 10 with 51:11, and may be part of the work of Isaiah of Babylon. Some think it is an even later statement of prophetic-apocalyptic hope. The lectionary focuses on 35:5-6a. Such healings were taken to be part of the age-to-come in Jewish thought (2 Esd. 7:53 [123]; 8:52-53; Jub. 23:26-30). In Isaiah 35 it is assumed that it is God who will do these things. "To sing for joy" (v. 6; cf. 35:1a, 2, 10) is a leitmotif of this "great day coming" that Jesus' miracles specifically herald. The infirm and feeble will make it into God's presence, with rejoicing, thanks to God. (Bodily healing seems intended, but cf. also Isa. 42:7, 18-20; 43:8 on the people as blind and deaf but liberated by God from spiritual bondage.)

SECOND LESSON: JAMES 1:17-27

Some four or (in the *Ordo*) five weeks in the Letter of James begin with this typical section of miscellaneous but practical advice, grounded in God the Father (1:17, 27) as creator and birthgiver. The *Ordo* is here a week ahead of L, E, and CL, but the others catch up by combining 2:1-5 and 2:14-18 (*Ordo* Pentecost 16 and 17) on Pentecost 17. The diatribe on faith and works (2:14-26) will thus be represented in the readings only briefly. Lectionary omission of the brief salutation (1:1, James to the twelve tribes in the Dispersion) and of 1:2-16 on trials and tribulations (*peirasmos*, same word in Greek, vv. 2, 12; cf. vv. 13-14) might be alluded to in setting the stage for the preaching text.

The author of this NT "wisdom book" is still taken by some to be a brother of Jesus who became a Christian leader, even "bishop," in Jerusalem (James B. Adamson, NICNT 1976; *James the Man and His Message* [Grand Rapids: Eerdmans, 1989]); by many more commentators to be an unknown Jewish Christian with a polished Greek style, A.D. 70–100 (M. Dibelius and H. Greeven, Hermeneia 1976; S. Laws, HNTC 1980). Still others assume materials from the martyred James the Just, between A.D. 40 and 62, redacted by a later editor (P. H. Davids, NIGTC 1982; R. P. Martin, WBC 48, 1988). For overviews, see T. W. Leahy, *NJBC* #58; *VU* 189–202; S. Laws, *ABD* 3:621-28; *TINT* 109–12 (#22). The overall tone of James may seem moralistic, much like the way a biographer summed up

Harry Truman as one who "held to the old guidelines: work hard, do your best, speak the truth, assume no airs, trust in God, have no fear" (D. McCullough, *Truman* [New York: Simon & Schuster, 1992], 991). But many aspects of James prove surprising.

The RC and L readings skip over 1:23-25, but these verses help one understand the key phrase "doers of the word" (1:22) and begin to introduce James's particular understanding of "the law [of liberty]" (1:25), which will be developed in the next week's epistle lesson. Verses 17-19 offer a brief characterization of the known character of God. The divine giving of gifts is stressed in v. 17a (in Greek a poetic hexameter line); "from above" and "coming down" (to us) are the operative additions. God's description as "Father of lights" stresses lordship over the universe in terms of its stars and heavenly luminaries (Gen. 1:3; Isa. 45:6,7; Job 38:4-33) and paves the way for describing in astrological terms God's unchangeableness of purpose (v. 17b; textual variants abound, but the main point is clear).

It was God's will to give us birth. Choice of the verb here (*apekyesen*, often used of a mother) reflects 1:15, about how desire in a person gives birth to sin. God's counteraction is bringing us to life as "a kind of first fruits" of all creatures. The most common interpretation applies v. 18 to the rebirth of Christian converts through baptism (cf. 1 Pet. 1:3, 23; John 1:12-13; 3:3-5). But the creation context ("Father of lights"; "first fruits" in the harvest festival, Lev. 23:10-14; but cf. 1 Cor. 15:20) suggests also the creation of humankind. The paraphrase in CEV, God "wanted us to be his own special people," further implies a reference to Israel (cf. Deut. 32:8-9); then the Law or Torah would be "the word of truth" (Ps. 119:43). The Israel reference seems least likely; one should look to both creation and new birth by the word or gospel as the basis for what follows.

What the beloved are to understand unfolds rapidly. Verse 19 includes admonitions to "brilliant listening" (to others and to the word) and "eloquent silence" (A. T. Robertson, *Practical and Social Aspects of Christianity: The Wisdom of James* [New York: G. H. Doran, 1915], 87–92) and to put the brakes on "dull anger," which does not produce (v. 20) "God's righteousness" (Matt. 6:33, what God's will calls for). In v. 21, "rid yourselves" or "put off" suggests baptismal language ethically applied (Eph. 4:22, 25), here to vulgarity and malice that threaten relationships in life. How can one receive "the implanted word"? By that is meant not something innate in all people but the word heard at conversion/baptism, which, for salvation, must be received and accepted humbly (cf. 3:13) and acted on or internalized.

The problem is that many people merely hear; they do not *do* the word (v. 22). They are like those who take a quick look in a mirror and go away forgetting what has been revealed (vv. 23-24). The "law of liberty," which involves the "implanted word" in its totality (as indicative: what God has given us; and imperative: the divine will) calls for persevering response. Blessed will be those who act on what they know from God (v. 25). The final paragraph (vv. 26-27) moves on beyond words to deeds via the term "religion" (*thrēskeia*, normally "cultic obligations"; Acts 26:5; Col. 2:18, "worship"). James picks out two criteria for proper "cult" before God (cf. Rom. 12:1): (1) care for oppressed groups without champions (the two examples, orphans and widows, were prominent in antiquity; Isa. 1:10-17; Ezek. 22:7; Deut. 14:29) and (2) a point overlooked by activists: not letting "this world make you evil" (CEV). James's view of the world is not a positive or friendly one (4:4), for there sin and death corrupt (1:14-15; cf. 4:13—5:6). This position is like that in the Fourth Gospel (1:10-11; 15:18-25; 16:8-11; 17:14-16) or Paul (Rom. 3:9-12; 1 Cor. 11:32; cf. Eph. 2:2). Søren Kierkegaard brought James into prominence to drive hearers from religiosity to true and full religion.

GOSPEL: MARK 7:31-37

All four Gospels include miracle stories; Mark has some nineteen of them. They are often clustered, as in 1:21—2:12 (appointed for Epiphany 4–7), or in the fivefold collections (of three healings, a feeding, and a sea story) in 4:35—6:44 and in 6:45—8:26, of which this graphic healing in 7:31-37 of a deaf man with a speech impediment is a part. In lectionary readings no miracle stories have been assigned since Pentecost 5 (4:35-41, storm at sea) and Pentecost 6 (Jairus's daughter and/or the woman with hemorrhages in 5:21-43). Out of the ten miracles in Mark 4:35—8:26, only two or three have thus been read, plus the feeding of the five thousand in its Johannine version, and now 7:31-37, the healing of a hearing- and speech-impaired person. It functions in Mark at several levels of meaning.

The account opens with an overly precise geographical itinerary in v. 31 that brings Jesus from Tyre to the Decapolis, from one Gentile region to another. The route is inexact, like going from New York to Philadelphia via Boston. It serves to frame the story about the Syrophoenician woman who asked for exorcism of a demon from her daughter (7:24-30) by means of references to Tyre (vv. 24, 31). If the stories about the woman's faith and a deaf man's healing by Jesus did not earlier circulate together (as some think), Mark has brought them together as a pair.

The story of the man deaf and unable to speak intelligibly begins abruptly: They (family? friends?) brought him to Jesus (who goes unnamed in vv. 32-37). The characteristic features in a healing miracle are present: description of illness (v. 32); means of care (vv. 33-34); result (v. 35). The account is unusually detailed and at points comparable only to 8:22-26 (the blind man of Bethsaida). Jesus takes the deaf person apart from the crowd (v. 33; cf. 5:37, 40; 8:23). This could have been out of respect for the man's privacy or to avoid curious stares. But it may also point to the secrecy theme in v. 36 or reflect a habit of Jesus (4:34 "in private"; 6:31-32). The method of healing involves placing fingers in the man's ears and the use of spittle (v. 33). Spit was often regarded as therapeutic in antiquity, like water, wine, or oil. Vespasian was asked by a blind man in Alexandria to moisten his eyelids with the emperor's spit (Tacitus, *Histories* 4.81; cf. John 9:6-7). Besides touching, Jesus looked heavenward, sighed (probably a gesture of prayer), and employed an Aramaic phrase still preserved in our Greek (and English) accounts. The man's ears and tongue were thus healed. A hint of exorcism is suggested in the loosing of the "bond" or "string" of his tongue (KJV, bound by Satan?).

Verse 36 reflects what has been called in Mark the "messianic secret": Tell no one (cf. 5:43; 8:26; 9:30; see below, on Pentecost 18). It works no better here than in some other passages, such as 1:44-45, because of a second factor: crowd reaction. They proclaim the event. While the command by Jesus could be taken to refer only to the means of cure, or as a reflection of his desire to work "in private," apart from publicity, the theme belongs with the very nature of a Gospel: that who Jesus was (known in part from what he did) had to become apparent only after cross and resurrection (1:23-25, 34; 8:30; 9:9). The closing words of admiration and acclamation from the crowd that would not keep silence (v. 37) evoke Gen. 1:31 (God saw what had been made or done was good—echoes of a new creation) and Sir. 39:16.

The attention in this story is on Jesus. It reflects his uncanny power to heal and exorcise demons. The Hellenistic church may have seen him as a divine wonderworker, working by means of what for Greeks was a foreign formula (*Ephphatha*, v. 34) to heal. But there is another level. Only here and in Isa. 35:5-6 is the term *mogilalos* used (for the deaf man, "scarcely speaking, with an impediment, speechless"). This story, like others, portrays Jesus as God's eschatological agent who opens the eyes of the blind and the ears of the deaf and the tongue of the speechless, as Isaiah promised for a future day. Jesus' activity heralds God's new age. (The OT reading reinforces this.) Alas, the disciples are portrayed as obtuse to the true significance (6:52; 8:17-18). In 8:27-35 (Pentecost 17) they will begin to see; 8:22-26 (blind man cured) sets the stage for Peter's confession, as does 7:36-37. Who is Jesus . . . for us?

Seventeenth Sunday after Pentecost

Lutheran	Roman Catholic	Episcopal	Common Lectionary
Isa. 50:4-10	Isa. 50:5-9a	Isa. 50:4-9	Prov. 22:1-2, 8-9
James 2:1-5, 8-10, 14-18	James 2:14-18	James 2:1-5, 8-10, 14-18	James 2:1-5, 8-10, 14-18
Mark 8:27-35	Mark 8:27-35	Mark 8:27-38	Mark 8:27-38

FIRST LESSON: ISAIAH 50:4-10

Most of the third Servant Song by Isaiah of Babylon (50:4-9) is used by RC, E, and L lectionaries to relate to the Gospel reading on Jesus as the teacher (Mark 8:34-38) who responds to Peter's confession at Caesarea Philippi (Mark 8:27-29) by teaching how, as the Son of Man, he must suffer and be killed (vv. 30-33). A "suffering servant" typology is thus intended by the lectionary, even though modern scholars debate whether Jesus saw himself as "the Servant" (cf. *TINT* 2.7; 7.5). The passage is part of the work of "the Second Isaiah" (chaps. 40–55) and has for the past century been labeled one of the four Servant Songs, with 42:1-7, 49:1-7, and 52:13—53:12.

Exact identification of this servant of the Lord continues to be debated, whether Israel or a portion of the nation or an individual, such as the prophet or the Persian king Cyrus (45:1; cf. *NJBC* 21:6). One recent analysis distinguishes Israel as the servant in 40:1—49:4 (specifically so in 41:8-10; 44:1-2; 48:20); Cyrus (and his successors Darius and Artaxerxes) as Yahweh's anointed shepherd (44:26, 28; 45:1); and the plural, "servants of Yahweh," in 54:17 (cf. 65:13-16) for God's believing, obedient worshipers. Moreover, John D. W. Watts (*Isaiah 34–66* [WBC 25, 1987], 115–18, 193–204, 227–29) separates "the servant passages" from the specifically "sufferer/martyr passages" of 50:4-9 and chapter 53, and sets our verses amid the events at Jerusalem in 522 B.C. when Zerubbabel (Ezra 3:2; Zechariah 1–8) was seeking to rebuild the temple. Isaiah 50:4-9 would then enunciate the vision and faith of, and pressures on, this Davidic leader who likely was extinguished by opponents. On this reconstruction, Darius responds in v. 10 to the servant leader's words in vv. 4-9.

In antiquity, however, no one treated "servant songs" in isolation from the Book of Isaiah as a whole, and there was less attention to a *suffering servant* (let alone "messiah") than Christians suppose. Much is made after Easter of such a paradox, however, by 1 Peter (2:21, 24) and Acts (3:13,

26). "Servant" verses were applied more *to* Jesus than spoken *by* him (chiefly at Luke 22:37 = Isa. 53:12). But traditional church usage readily referred most of the Isaiah verses to Jesus. In 50:4 (where E and L begin the unit) the exilic period (or Jerusalem in 522 B.C.) is reflected in the need "to sustain the weary with a word" (true of Jesus as a comforter but hardly at Caesarea Philippi). The speaker appears as a disciple with disciples ("those who are taught," RSV twice; NRSV too quickly conjectures "teacher" for the speaker—one must learn before teaching). Jesus appears expressly as teacher in Mark 8:31. This ready pupil (50:5) faces opposition (vividly depicted in v. 6 as beatings and humiliation; cf. Neh. 13:25 on "debearding" as an insult, and Matt. 5:39 and Mark 10:34 for reflections of such language). But the prophet trusts in God who vindicates the faithful (50:7-8; Jesus in Mark 8:31 expects a humiliating death, then divine vindication). Firm as flint, he sets his face in confidence toward God and in his own mission (50:7b, 8-9, God in contrast to adversaries who will wear out like a moth-eaten garment). But the precise outcome is left open. The stance is like that of Jeremiah (cf. Jer. 11:20; 20:7-8, 11-12), but the servant views such vicious hatred and abuse and his acceptance of it as revelation of what God wills (50:5-6; 53:4, 6, 10). Small wonder that 50:4-7 is read on Passion/Palm Sunday all three years in the *Ordo*. By adding v. 10, L provides the only direct reference to God's "servant" in the passage. A narrator asks who follows in the train of the servant by so trusting God, no matter what. The Gospel for the day says Jesus does, and asks the same of his disciples.

The CL continues its readings in wisdom materials with four separate examples from *Proverbs 22* of "sentence literature." They concern (v. 1) reputation as preferable over wealth; (v. 2) our creaturehood under God, whether rich or poor; (v. 8) how sowing injustice reaps evil; and (v. 9) sharing with the poor. These aphorisms are best related to the epistle for the day, perhaps used to spur justice and generosity (cf. Gal. 6:7; 2 Cor. 9:7), without claiming to explain wealth and poverty.

SECOND LESSON: JAMES 2:1-5, 8-10, 14-18

Each of these short excerpts could form the basis for a powerful message. James 2:1-5 (RC, Pentecost 16) sketches a scene of discrimination among religious people, favoring the rich over the poor, so starkly that little comment is needed, only application. The opening verse asks whether (NRSV; or states that, NRSV note, RSV) "acts of favoritism" (or partiality) are compatible with faith in Jesus Christ. The closing word in v. 1, literally "of the glory," can be taken as a modifier, "our glorious Lord" (NRSV), or with Christ (cf. RSV, NEB), or even as a title, the Glory (or Shekinah), the presence of God in Jesus.

48

Verse 1 is the most significantly Christian note in James and defines the object of faith (Jesus) as well as details in what follows. The "assembly" (v. 2, *synagōgē*) suggests a gathering of Jewish Christians for worship; the "footstool" (v. 3, NRSV note), furniture in a synagogue denoting a place of little honor (Pss. 99:5; 110:1; Matt. 5:35). The phrase in v. 4, "judges with evil thoughts," however, suggests to some an assembly for judicial purposes, and so a reflection of Lev. 19:15 (do "not be partial to the poor or defer to the great; with justice you shall judge your neighbor"), encouraged by quotation of Lev. 19:18 a few verses later at 2:8. Mr. Gold Rings has been identified as a Roman knight of senatorial rank or the pagan master where a house church meets or a rich Jew; both he and Mr. or Ms. Shabby are visitors, new converts, or litigants. The setting is unclear; but the main point is crystal clear: no favoritism should be shown to rich over poor.

The principle in v. 5, a favorite in liberation theology, falls midway between the versions of Jesus' beatitude about the poor in Luke 6:20 (economically poor in contrast to the rich, 6:24) and in Matt. 5:3 ("poor in spirit"). It is here literal poverty ("dirty clothes") but not poverty as a virtue in itself, for it is characterized by faith and love (v. 5bc). Verses 6-7 (not assigned) list experiences with the rich that make siding with them against the poor the more heinous. Elsa Tamez (*The Scandalous Message of James* [New York: Crossroad, 1990], 30–32) even thinks James did not favor opening the church to the rich (yet cf. 5:1-11). How to live, not who is excluded, is at issue.

Verses 8-10 (and 11-13) can be regarded as the theological underpinning for the vignettes in vv. 1-5 about partiality to the rich and the words in vv. 14-18 about the naked and hungry. To show partiality, even under the guise of love for (some) neighbors (Lev. 19:18), violates other parts of the "royal" law of God's kingdom, 19:15 (above), for example. The premise that one is obligated to keep the whole law and not do one commandment while ignoring others (v. 11) is found in Paul (Gal. 3:10; 5:3) and indeed in the Torah itself (Deut. 27:26). The need to uphold the whole law, without favoritism but with mercy (cf. Matt. 5:7), is underscored by impending judgment. As at 1:25, there is here a view of the law as "perfect," "liberating," centered upon the love command, and marked by mercy. It forgoes judging the neighbor (4:11-12). Such a view is different from Judaism, Paul, or later forms of Christianity and assumes "law" to be part of the "word of truth" that sets forth God's will for human life as expressed in OT commandments (2:11) and in Jesus' teachings (cf. L. Goppelt, *Theology of the New Testament* [Grand Rapids: Eerdmans] 2 [1982]: 199–211; *VU* 198–99).

James's "ethic of justice" continues with another example of how religious people fall short when they say they have faith (2:1, 5, 14) but are not "doers of the word" (1:22; 2:14). When confronted by fellow Christians (a brother or a sister, v. 15) who need clothes and food, they dismiss them with pious, even liturgical platitudes, "Depart in peace," "May God supply your needs." This is a caricature of living, active faith. James does not say whether one should give the shirt off one's back personally (cf. Matt. 5:40) or participate in a relief committee, but somehow to express faith through deeds is the point (v. 17). Works show that faith exists (v. 18). That is all the lectionary reading calls for.

Verses 19-26 go on to castigate mere intellectual belief (v. 19), with OT examples of faith active in works. Since one of these is Abraham in Gen. 15:6 (v. 23, a verse Paul also cited to show justification by faith [Gal. 3:6-9; Romans 4]) and since James 2:24 uses "faith alone" (a phrase never actually found in Paul), treatments usually seek to bring these verses into relation with Paul. Each faces different situations. James and Paul are complementary, James writing simplistically to prevent misunderstandings of Paul, whether during his lifetime (Adamson 1989: 195–227) or more likely on the part of later Paulinists (Laws, HNTC 129–33; VU 199–201). Davids (131–33) assumes people who say, "We believe; don't bother us further, especially about charity." The facts are that faith alone saves (cf. Paul, and John 6, above), but faith can never be alone (James) in a world of needs. The preacher can in 2:14-18 concentrate on faith's responses to hunger and other crying needs but also to discrimination (2:1-5); with support from a view of the word that includes God's will expressed in the law of the kingdom (2:8-10).

GOSPEL: MARK 8:27-38

After several readings in Mark on miracles (Pentecost 5, 6, 16) and teachings (Pentecost 2, 3, 4, 8, 15) and occasional narratives (Pentecost 7, 9), we come to a watershed incident, Peter's confession of Jesus as Messiah at Caesarea Philippi (8:27-30). It is followed by the first passion prediction (v. 31), the rebuke of Peter in the "Satan saying" (vv. 32-33), and teachings on discipleship (vv. 34-35). This is extended in E and CL to include similar teachings in vv. 36-37 and an eschatological saying in v. 38. No lectionary includes the difficult eschatological statement in 9:1 that "some standing here . . . will not taste death until they see that the kingdom has come with power."

The passage is a watershed in that most of Mark prior to this peak was teaching about the kingdom of God, directed to the crowds, and was accompanied by many miracles (1—8:26), while the subsequent chapters will more and more concern Jesus' passion and resurrection, teachings addressed to disciples, with but occasional miracles (9:14-28; 10:46-52 only). There have been previous pointers to the passion in Mark (2:20; 3:6; 6:14-29), but none of these are read in the lectionary (though note John 6:14, 51c). Since the second passion prediction (9:31) will crop up next week, the preacher may wish to hold that emphasis and the disciples' uncompromising reaction until Pentecost 18. It should be noted that the Matthean account—where Peter is a hero of faith and his confession is matched by Jesus' confession, "You are Peter and upon this rock . . ." and words about the church (Matt. 16:17-19)—is not only read in Year A (Pentecost 14 and 15) but also assigned in two parts (16:13-20 and 21-26), thus separating Peter's confession and the Satan saying.

Interpretation of 8:27—9:1 in previous editions of *Proclamation* mirrors trends in recent decades of exegesis. The goal of commentators has often been to identify Mark's redactional emphases, a possible pre-Markan source, and then what likely happened in the life of Jesus (for a succinct example, see Fuller, *Preaching*, 425–26, or J. Reumann, *Jesus in the Church's Gospels* [Fortress Press, 1968], 264–65, 268–69 and notes). More recently in narrative approaches it has been popular to expound the book as it stands, in a literary manner, with little concern for "what happened." Inasmuch as the lectionary assigned all three Synoptic accounts (Luke 9:18-24 in Year C, Pentecost 5) and the Johannine equivalent of Peter's confession (John 6:69) just three weeks ago, the teacher-preacher is compelled to deal at least with the meaning in each book or evangelist. Listeners are apt to recall other versions as Mark's is read, however, and so historical questions may call for treatment too.

The basic narrative in 8:27-29 has as its immediate context the healing of a blind person at Bethsaida, who comes to see only in stages (8:22-26); many take this as a foil to the disciples in vv. 27-33, Peter included, who have not yet come to see who Jesus really is. Morna Hooker's title for 8:27-30 is a bit over-optimistic, "The Disciples' Eyes Are Opened" (*Mark*, 199–203), for here, as in next week's reading, "they did not understand" (9:32). Near the villages of the Caesarea of Herod Philip, north of Galilee, Jesus asks the disciples about public opinion concerning him. Every answer pegs him as a prophet (no mean title, since prophets had been lacking in Israel for centuries). People compare him to Elijah (expected to come again, 9:11-12) or the recently martyred John the Baptist. Then to Jesus' second question—your opinion?—Peter responds, "You are the Messiah" (NRSV rightly uses the Hebrew term for the Greek *Christos*, "anointed one").

Verse 30 does not offer congratulations to Peter from Jesus but a rebuke to keep silent (cf. 1:44; 5:43). Instead, Jesus openly begins to talk about how "the Son of Man" faces suffering and death at the hands of the authorities and then resurrection (from God) (vv. 31-32a). Peter flares up at such talk, rebuking Jesus for this note of suffering (v. 32). Jesus in turn rebukes Peter as an adversary of God, on the side of human aims (v. 33). The narrative, as it stands, has rightly been called Peter's tragic misunderstanding of Jesus as a heroic human figure; for Peter, suffering is anathema. Peter had in mind the Messiah as a military leader (as in the *Psalms of Solomon*, chap. 17, and the Zealot movement). Jesus silences (v. 30) and corrects (v. 31) such a demonic (cf. v. 33, satanic) misunderstanding. Only slowly, and ultimately after Easter, will the disciples come to understand aright what "Messiah" is meant to mean—a suffering Son of Man.

Verses 34-35 begin to apply such a self-understanding of Jesus to disciples: Followers are to deny self, take up crosses (a not uncommon sight in Palestine, quite apart from Jesus' passion); they are to use and lose themselves for Jesus' sake. Mark adds in a phrase uniquely his own, "and for the sake of the gospel" (cf. 10:29), thus identifying Jesus and the good news. Verses 36-37 continue this sense of giving oneself ("soul," life) for the cause and person of Jesus. These are wisdom sayings (like "You can't take it with you") made Christian by context (Jesus, not worldly gain, saves). Verse 38 brings in the necessary eschatological note: True meanings will become apparent at the final judgment; one's relation to Jesus now, unashamedly, will determine eternal destiny then.

This is a rich passage. One could focus on Jesus. In v. 30 the closing words "about him" are a clue. The verses call for a proper understanding and confession of the crucified and risen one; they call for life, service, and salvation for Jesus' sake. Or the focus could be on Peter—here an impetuous follower who does not yet understand that, for Jesus, messiahship means suffering and service (cf. 10:45). Peter's incorrect confession of Jesus will become a proper one only later, when suffering as the way to lordship is grasped. The focus could also be on us as disciples (vv. 34-38), learning to gain the mind of Jesus, which means self-giving before glory.

Eighteenth Sunday after Pentecost

Lutheran	Roman Catholic	Episcopal	Common Lectionary
Jer. 11:18-20	Wisd. 2:12, 17-20	Wisd. 1:16—2:1, 12-22	Job 28:20-28
James 3:16—4:6	James 3:16—4:3	James 3:16—4:6	James 3:13-18
Mark 9:30-37	Mark 9:30-37	Mark 9:30-37	Mark 9:30-37

FIRST LESSON: WISDOM OF SOLOMON 1:16—2:1, 12-22

The *Ordo* originally appointed Wisd. 2:12, 17-20 (which E expanded), on "the righteous man," God's "child" whom opponents seek to bring to "a shameful death." This picture of a "righteous sufferer" in Wisdom 1–2 (and 3:1, 4, 8-9; 5:1-2, 4), in a document from the first century B.C., provides a link between the "suffering servant" in Isaiah and Jesus, including the picture of Christ in Phil. 2:6-11. In churches not reading deutero-canonical books at worship, alternatives are assigned (see below).

The Book of Wisdom, attributed to Solomon (cf. Wisd. 9:8; 7:1-14 and 8:17—9:18 with 1 Kings 3:6-9), was composed sometime after 50 B.C. in Egypt by a Jew who had long meditated on the OT writings and Greek philosophy. He wrote this Greek treatise, likely in Alexandria, in the face of Jews who had left their religion for a life-style of the day that urged "Might makes right" (2:11), "Gather ye rosebuds while ye may" (Robert Herrick; cf. 2:8), and "Get all the gusto that you can" (cf. 2:7, 9). No God, no judgment (2:1b-5), no need therefore to be just (2:10)! The author describes them as "ungodly" persons who have made a pact with death (1:16) and reasoned wrongly that existence ends with death (2:1). He himself believes God will give immortality (3:4; 15:3; through wisdom, 8:13; resurrection of the body is unmentioned, unless by implication at 16:13). This gift depends on one's relationship with God.

The "righteous poor man," whom these godless enemies want to do in because he is an inconvenient reminder of God (2:10, 12-20), claims to be God's child or servant (2:13; *pais*), with God his father (2:16). The RC reading focuses on what the opponents say. The E reading adds more of the setting (1:16—2:1), contents of the righteous servant's living reproof of sin (2:12-16), and the contrast between God's purposes and human wickedness. Jesus, in Mark 9:30, similarly looks to God's vindication (cf. Wisd. 3:2-9) after death. But it is unlikely he was influenced by this Alexandrian Greek book any more than he was by Plato's words, "The just man will have to endure the lash, the rod, chains, the branding-iron in his eyes, and finally . . . he will be crucified" (*Republic* 361E).

Lutheran (and initially Presbyterian and Methodist) lectionaries substituted one of *Jeremiah*'s "confessions" (11:18-20; cf., e.g., 12:1-6; 15:10-21). These deeply personal prayer laments have been compared to the Isaianic Servant poems; note "like a gentle lamb led to the slaughter" (11:19) and Isa. 53:7. In Matt. 16:14 (Caesarea Philippi) Jeremiah was one of the prophets to whom people were comparing Jesus. Without claiming that this forensic complaint by Jeremiah was formative for Jesus or the evangelists, we can compare and contrast the mood and outlook.

The prophet Jeremiah knew from God (11:18) of his calling and mission (1:5-10). Now, perhaps in 594 B.C., he reaps opposition, even from his hometown neighbors in Anathoth (11:21) and his own family (12:6; cf. Mark 6:1-6), for the words of judgment (more on "plucking up" and "pulling down" than on "building up," 1:10; 45:4) that he proclaimed concerning Israel's disobedience to God's covenant (11:1-17, esp. 8-9, 11, 14). The people were once God's "green olive tree" with "goodly fruit" (11:16). They now scheme to destroy Jeremiah ("the tree with its fruit"), cutting off his life and even his name (v. 19). Jesus the prophet foresees a similar fate for himself (Mark 9:31; cf. Luke 23:31) but does not call for the retribution for which Jeremiah prays (v. 20; cf. 1 Pet. 2:23). The lectionary omits the grim affirmation of this wish by God in 11:22-23 and the words of scant comfort in 12:5. Worse is yet to come for the prophet.

The CL substitutes *Job 28:20-28* for either the reference to the righteous sufferer in Wisdom 2 or to Jeremiah as a type of Jesus. Job can be claimed as a democratized version of the prophet-priest Jeremiah and his experience, but the reading seems not to be connected with Mark 9 by the Free Church lectionary makers, but at most with James 3 on wisdom "from above." Or 28:20-28 can be proclaimed in its own right, on divine wisdom as revealed, with a closing moral touch in v. 28. (See recent commentaries by N. C. Habel [Philadelphia: Westminster, 1985]; J. G. Janzen [Int. 1985]; D. J. A. Clines [WBC 17, 1989]; and J. H. Hartley [NICOT, 1988]).

SECOND LESSON: JAMES 3:16—4:6

More wisdom teaching for ethical living is provided in these units from James. They develop previous themes in the document in practical ways for a community and individuals trying to be faithful to God in a world where the devil is at work (4:7, part of next Sunday's epistle, except in the RC *Ordo*). The theme of care about words in speech (cf. 1:19; 2:3—

4:12, 14-16) is applied to teachers (3:1) and then to all of us (3:2-12) in a monitory passage about the power of the tongue, which all four lectionaries omit. Only CL includes 3:13-15, about those truly wise among the community members. Their conduct and words (2:14-26) exhibit "gentleness" (3:13; cf. 3:17 and 1:21 "meekness"), which comes through wisdom from God (1:5, 17). Indeed, two kinds of wisdom are presented, earthly (v. 15) and that from above (v. 17). Their contrast reminds one of passages in Paul (1 Cor. 1:21-25, 27-31; 3:18-20) but already was suggested in OT and Jewish writings (Prov. 2:6-19; 8:22-31; Sir. 1:1-10; Wisd. 7:24-28). The results of the lack of true wisdom are put in personal (v. 14) and political (v. 16) terms: envy and ambition lead to disorder (*akatastasia* can mean anarchy, even revolution), and all sorts of evils. The adjectives used to describe the two kinds of wisdom are worth checking in commentaries (e.g., R. P. Martin, WBC 48:131–38).

By beginning with 3:16, RC, L, and E pick up with the results of devilish wisdom and then see in v. 17 the characterization of heavenly wisdom, without the full contrast outlined above. But links to previous chapters can be seen in the reference to mercy (2:13), avoidance of partiality (2:1, "favoritism"), and "good fruits" (2:14-18, "works"). In 3:18 a positive result from true wisdom is set forth (in contrast to vv. 14 and 16): for peacemakers (NRSV text; cf. Matt. 5:9) the fruit or result of what God's righteousness calls for and what heavenly wisdom provides is peaceable conduct sown by God.

In the zigs and zags of James's treatise, a rhetorically polished unit follows. James 4:1-6 begins with two direct questions (v. 1) and is continued by a rhythmic castigation of those addressed in the second person (vv. 2-3); it reaches a climax in another question to this audience of "adulteresses" (v. 4) and is clinched by scriptural citation(s) about God (vv. 5-6) who is the behind-the-scenes figure throughout most of the document. Another genealogy-like passage (cf. 1:14-16; 3:16) here argues that it is cravings or desires that produce conflicts and disputes (RSV, "wars and fightings"). The reference to desires "at war within you" may suggest the divided soul of an individual (S. Laws, *James*, HNTC, 168), but "you" is plural throughout, and so a (church) community seems intended (Davids, 155–56).

The thought becomes clearer in the structuring suggested by Dibelius and Greeven (p. 218) for vv. 2-3 (in NRSV's words):

> you want something—and do not have it;
>   so you commit murder.
> you covet something—and cannot obtain it;
>   so you engage in disputes and conflicts.
> you do not have—because you do not ask;
> you ask—and do not receive
>   because you ask wrongly.

At this point the theme becomes prayer (cf. 1:5-7; Matt. 7:7-9), and the RC reading ends on this note. But vv. 4:4-6 (E, L) go on to speak about the God addressed in prayer. It is an either/or. Friendship with "the world" means one is an enemy of God. The thought, uncongenial as it is to many moderns, elaborates on 1:27c and 3:6 ("a world of iniquity," not to mention sin and death, 1:15). James means specifically the world of human beings, perverse, lusting, marked by selfish ambitions (3:14, 16; 4:1-3). The feminine form of "adulterer" reflects biblical usage by the prophets for Israel's unfaithfulness to God her "husband" (Jer. 3:20; Hos. 9:1; Isa. 1:21; 57:3) and by Jesus (Mark 8:38). James seeks to tie the argument together by a reminder in v. 6 of grace given (cf. 1:17-18) to the humble (Prov. 3:34, LXX; cf. the emphasis on "meekness" in 1:21; 3:13) and divine opposition to the proud (rich, 2:5; merciless, 2:13; boastful, 3:14). The quotation in v. 5 is less clear as to meaning and origin (in the OT, Exod. 20:5 and 34:14 strike a similar tone, but it may be from a lost writing). The NRSV rendering means God seeks response from the spirit divinely placed in us, and this through prayer and faithful conduct.

What prompted these words of James in 3:18—4:6? Perhaps he was addressing disputes in the church community, maybe involving teachers (3:1). Why then the references to wars (4:1) and murder (4:2)? Hence some (B. Reicke, AB 37:4–6, 45–46; R. P. Martin, WBC 48:143–45, 156–57) see the passage directed against the Zealots (4:2 "covet" = zēloute, you are zealous). The Zealot answer was violence in the world and even revolution (3:16, "disorder"). The Zealot option is, for James, not God's will.

GOSPEL: MARK 9:30-37

Déja vu! The reading seems a rerun of last week's. Again on the way through Galilee (to Jerusalem), in secrecy (9:30, Jesus "did not want any one to know"; cf. 8:30), Jesus makes a second prediction of the passion to the disciples (9:31; cf. 8:31). They do not understand (9:32), any more than Peter did in 8:31-32 about a suffering Son of Man. When they arrive at Capernaum (9:33-34), Jesus asks what they had been arguing about en route; they do not own up that it was about who of them was greatest, so Jesus must teach them again that to be first means to be servant of all (9:35; cf. 8:34-37). As illustration, Jesus takes a little child in his arms but instead of saying that disciples must be childlike or receive the kingdom like a child (cf. 10:13-16), he speaks of how welcoming such a child is like welcoming Jesus himself and the One who sent him (9:36-37). A passion announcement, uncomprehending disciples, and teachings about servanthood are themes that will also resound in 10:33-34 (third passion prediction), 10:35-40 (James and John seek places of glory in the kingdom to come), and 10:43-45 (servanthood, like the Son of Man), most of which is the Gospel assigned for Pentecost 22.

The original disciples in Mark's story needed more than two reruns to grasp the shattering message that the Son of Man must suffer and die (8:31-33; 9:31-32; 10:32-40); in spite of the clarity of 10:45, they will all desert him in the garden (14:50), Peter will thrice deny he even knew Jesus (14:66-72), and none of them will be around to hear the news the frightened women failed to tell (16:8). This repetition of themes in 9:30-37 gives the teacher in each preacher an opportunity to reiterate and deepen some key points.

In v. 30b the "messianic secret" is reflected. This term is broadly used to cover (1) incognito journeys as here and at 7:24 (cf. also the withdrawls at 6:31, 53-54; 7:17, 24, 31; 8:27; 9:2; 10:1); (2) the command, after a healing, to tell no one (1:44; 5:43; 7:36; 8:26); (3) prohibitions to demoniacs that demons not identify him (cf. 1:23-26; 5:7-13; 9:25-27); (4) the parables as "the secret of the kingdom" (4:10-12); and (5) the disciples' lack of understanding about a suffering Messiah/Son of Man (as here in 9:32). These features have been attributed to Mark the evangelist to account for the assumption that Mark's source material was originally unmessianic; Mark covered this by suggesting that Jesus wanted his messiahship to be kept secret (so W. Wrede, *The Messianic Secret*, trans. J. C. G. Greig [Cambridge/London: James Clarke, 1971; Greenwood, S. C.: Attic Press, 1971). Others trace the secrecy theme to the historical Jesus (V. Taylor, *Mark* [New York: St. Martin's Press, 1952], 122–24). Still others attribute it to early Christians, prior to Mark's redaction.

Actually, a variety of factors were at work in these features of Mark's Gospel. The "mystery of the kingdom" (number 4, above) is distinct from Jesus' identity and has to do in Mark with a way of reading the parable of the Sower (4:1-9) to fit the later church situation (4:13-20) for those ("you") who are "outside" the kingdom. Miracles (number 2) are only sometimes covered by a command to silence, which is in any case seldom observed (cf. 1:45 and 7:36-37 above). Numbers 3 and 5 go together: the supernatural world of Satan knows quite well that Jesus is God's chosen representative (1:11; 9:7) with power (1:27; 2:6-12; 3:27, stronger than the "strong man," Satan); but the disciples are slow to catch on. Eyes must be opened, eventually by the cross and God's raising of Jesus; faith is God's gift (*TINT* 125–26 [25.5]).

Is this preachable? Yes, in the way Mark narrates the disciples' story. Dull, undiscriminating, and afraid to ask (9:32), they are like many followers even in churches today. They want to be "number one" ("I'm the greatest"), and they need repeated instruction into the way of Jesus—even Peter (8:32) and James and John (10:35), who have "been to the mountain" with Jesus (9:2-8). Such instruction is provided here not only in the general admonition for followers about serving *all* others (v. 35, inclusivity) but also by v. 31, the passion prediction. This is briefer than those in 8:31 and 10:33-34, less a passion narrative and cast more in terms that the historical Jesus might have used.

His term "Son of Man" continues to be debated by biblical scholars, and attempts at inclusive language only obfuscate what was already a strange term in Greek ("the Man from Heaven" tilts too much toward an uncertain background in the Book of Enoch). All it need have meant in Aramaic was "this person, I" (Ps. 8:4; NRSV, "mortals")—yet with prophetic overtones (Ezek. 2:1; 36:1) and a note of vague mystery. For from Dan. 7:13-18 (NRSV, "one like a human being") came the sense of exaltation to dominion before the throne of God, the "Ancient One" (7:9, 13b). The Son of Man of whom Jesus speaks will be killed by human hands (specific Jewish authorities and the gentile Romans go unmentioned here). The resurrection that follows would be a more specific way of referring to the vindication by God that a trusting Jew like Jesus might expect (Ps. 22:1-5, 21b-22, 28-29; Wisd. 2:12-13, 18-23).

Have *we* learned to trust God with regard to the principles that discipleship is service and that faithfulness (and even suffering) is the way to life? One litmus test for Mark 9:35b is welcoming those who are little and defenseless, like a child (v. 37). The image shifts, however, to such children as the "little ones who believe in" Jesus (9:42, unfortunately read only in next week's lesson); whoever receives a disciple, receives Jesus and the God, as he says, "who sent me." Behind this saying is the Jewish principle that "the person sent has the authority of the master who sends him." That means Jesus as God's supreme representative, and believers as Jesus' representatives today. To be great in the kingdom is to welcome in Jesus' name, embrace (v. 37a), and serve all such in need with whom Jesus identifies. To be a disciple is to grasp who Jesus is and what God wills as "the way" in life. Church members and leaders, both, take note!

Nineteenth Sunday after Pentecost

Lutheran	Roman Catholic	Episcopal	Common Lectionary
Num. 11:4-6, 10-16, 24-29	Num. 11:25-29	Num. 11:4-6, 10-16, 24-29	Job 42:1-6
James 4:7-12	James 5:1-6	James 4:7-12	James 4:13-17; 5:7-11
Mark 9:38-50	Mark 9:38-50	Mark 9:38-50	Mark 9:38-50

FIRST LESSON: NUMBERS 11:4-6, 10-16, 24-29

These excerpts, from a basically J chapter about Israel in the wilderness, on the move from Sinai (10:11) toward the promised land (which scouts will reach in chap. 13), intertwine three stories loosely. They are framed by further stories of complaining in 11:1-3 and in chap. 12 (against Moses).

(1) Verses 11:4-10, 13, 18-23, and 31-35 tell of a revolt by "the riffraff" against the diet of manna and a "strong craving for" meat. Poor Moses! How will God's promise (v. 21) of meat for a month for 600,000 people be met? A wind from the Lord drops quail piled three feet high on the ground all around the camp. People gorge themselves until the meat comes out their ears (v. 20, "nostrils") and a plague strikes (v. 33). The place gets called "graves of craving" (v. 34, an *inclusio* or framing phrase with 11:4 "strong craving," Hebrew *taăwāh*). The story is reminiscent of Exod. 16:2-3, 11-15, on quail and manna (read at Pentecost 11) and of Exod. 15:22-26 and 17:1-7, complaints over water. But the lectionary tells only the first part of the quail story in Numbers 11, omitting the heaps of them and the plague.

(2) Verses 11-12, 14-17, and 24-25 contain an account of how Moses is overburdened with leadership and administration, unable to "carry all this people alone." So the Lord has him gather seventy elders from among the heads of families or officials; on them at the tent of meeting God puts "some of the spirit that was on" Moses, with the result that this one time the seventy "prophesied" (v. 25, ecstatic or frenzied outbursts, as in 1 Sam. 10:10-13; 19:20-24). This story is reminiscent of Exod. 18:13-27 (judges appointed to help Moses) and 24:19 (seventy elders), but the gift of spirit and its charismatic manifestation are new.

(3) In vv. 26-30 we learn that two men in the camp, who were not among the seventy at the tent, also received the spirit and prophesied. When Joshua (here, as in Exod. 33:11, not a military leader but Moses'

assistant, who stays always at the tent) heard this of Eldad and Medad, he wants Moses to stop them. The answer is no, Moses would have all God's people prophets! The *Ordo* concentrates solely on the seventy as prophets and then on Eldad and Medad. The E and L lectionaries add elements of the other stories: Craving for meat (vv. 4-6) leads to Moses' plaint before God, the divine appointment of the seventy, and, apart from them in the tent, two others in the camp similarly endowed with the spirit. The lectionary means this emphasis to be related to Mark 9:38-40: People outside "our group" of disciples or beyond official structures may be called and equipped by God for tasks like prophesying. The NT ultimately sees Num. 11:29 fulfilled at Pentecost (Acts 2:4, 17-18; 1 Cor. 12:13, 28-31). God's spirit is found in official leaders but may also be at work wherever God wills, outside normal structures (hence 1 Thess. 5:19; 1 Cor. 14:5; and Mark 9:39-40). The two Israelite outsiders live on, for example, in the Eldad-Medad ministry formed by the Rev. Ray Youngblood at St. Paul Community Baptist Church, Brooklyn, to supplement its board of elders. Bible study, group therapy, and fellowship on Tuesday nights help African American males in God's "recall on black men" (Samuel G. Freedman, *Upon This Rock: The Miracles of a Black Church* [New York: HarperCollins, 1991], 7–9, 58–63, 98, 273, 292, 301).

The CL prefers as its final wisdom passage Job's submission speech (*Job 42:1-6*), the last poetic verses of the Book of Job. God's voice out of the whirlwind (40:6—41:34) may be a better climax, for Job's words are somewhat pedestrian, as acknowledgment of God's powerful purpose. (Verses 42:3a and 4 are intrusive quotes of what God had said at 38:2, 3b; NAB omits.) Though Job has heard and "seen" God (God's concern and care for him), he ends in repentance. The preacher may wish to tell the prose story (chaps. 1–2; 42:7-17), give some idea of the wisdom of Job's "comforters," but finally dwell on Job's persistent faith (cf. James 5:11), met by encounter with God's manifestation of majesty, and a place in the creation as servant of God.

SECOND LESSON: JAMES 4:7-12

In L and E, last Sunday's reading is continued with the next six verses. RC skips from 4:3 to 5:1-6 for Pentecost 19. CL, having omitted 4:1-6, opts for 4:13-17 and 5:7-11. The content in every instance is parenetic, 4:7-12 and 5:7-11 offering a variety of general precepts, 4:13—5:6 more pointed social-ethical admonitions.

James 4:7-12 is rightly paragraphed in (N)RSV as two sections. The terms of address show this: "sinners" and "double-minded" in v. 8 for vv.

7-10, and "brothers and sisters" (*adelphoi*, Christians) in v. 11 for vv. 11-12. Yet presumably the same community of believers is involved, people of the new birth (1:18; 2:1) but in need of admonitions (2:1, 14, and throughout) to express faith by deeds (3:13). There is also a difference in content, for vv. 7-10 is a call to repent before God, while vv. 11-12 returns to the theme of speech within the community and not judging others (as in 3:1-12, teachers and the tongue; 2:1-9, no partiality; 2:13, mercy, not judgment). God (who has been the subject in 4:4-6) is mentioned at the beginning of the full reading, in 4:7-8a, and at its close, in 4:12, as lawgiver and judge "who is able to save and to destroy."

Verses 7-10 consist of ten imperatives, all of them decisive calls (regularly in the aorist tense) for disciples. With expository preaching at low ebb today, it is unlikely that preachers will opt for a ten-point sermon. But these summonses to what it means to live under grace (v. 6) do have a structure. The threefold sequence from Prov. 3:34 (in v. 6) and submission to God and resisting the devil also occur in 1 Pet. 5:5b-9. A common pattern is likely involved from catechetical instruction, as is suggested also by the verb "submit" (the same one discussed in Eph. 5:22 for the *Haustafeln*; see above, Pentecost 14). This idea is repeated in v. 10 ("Humble yourselves before the Lord," same term as in 4:6), so as to provide an overarching *inclusio* for vv. 7-10. But in 4:10 a promise is added: God will exalt you (cf. Luke 18:14).

In between vv. 7 and 10 the imperatives unfold in clusters of commands. If you resist the devil, this adversary of God will flee from you (cf. Eph. 6:11, 13; Jesus in Matt. 4:1-11). To do so is to "draw near to God," with the promise that God "will draw near to you" (v. 8; cf. Zech. 1:3). But the presence of God calls for purity; hence the call for repentance in v. 8b. Words like "draw near," "cleanse," and "purify" were originally cultic (Exod. 19:22; 30:19-21) but, as regularly in James (1:21, 26), have taken on moral and social meaning (as already in Ps. 24:4), such as is needed for "double-minded" sinners (cf. James 1:8). In them desires dominate (4:1) and they seek "the world" as well as God (4:4). Some, like R. P. Martin (WBC 48), see Zealot revolutionists here, who embrace war and killing, which is really "devilish" wisdom (3:15; 4:1-2; see Pentecost 18, closing comment, above). But all selfish ambition and desires that draw one from God are covered. In v. 9 prophetic imagery is employed to show the depths repentance may need to take (Jer. 4:8; Joel 2:12-13; Amos 8:10). All this is to lead to ultimate exaltation in the eschaton.

Verses 11-12 turn to brothers and sisters "talking down" or bad-mouthing others in the church. The argument takes an unexpected turn when it is said that such misuse of mouth and mind (3:8-12) also bad-mouths God's law, especially as 2:8-13 has described it (see above, Pentecost 17), centered in love for the neighbor. To judge other people (cf. Matt. 7:1) is also to judge God! The dominant emphasis is on God, the judge as well as lawgiver, who saves us but can also destroy.

The addition in CL of 4:13-17 to the reading provides the example of rich business people who make their plans (earthly wisdom!) without God and without the proviso "If the Lord wishes" (4:15, the *conditio Jacobaea*). The *Ordo* in 5:1-6 focuses solely on the unjust rich who rip off their farmworkers (5:4). It is of a piece with the social ethics (of liberation theology also) seen in 2:2-7. The "righteous one" in 5:6 (note "who does not resist you"; therefore nonviolence) might be a reference to Jesus (1 Pet. 3:18), but more likely reflects the figure of the innocent sufferer through the ages (Ps. 37:14, 32; Wisd. 2:12-20). By adding 5:7-11 to the pericope, CL gets in the new note of patient endurance and the familiar one of the eschatological judge (cf. 4:11-12). The "day of slaughter" (5:5; cf. Jer. 12:3) is God's day, not ours as Zealots. Those who preach wisely on James are urged to a balance of socially responsible calls for justice, especially in the church, and theologically responsible trust in God for the future.

GOSPEL: MARK 9:38-50

As already noted last week, this reading continues 9:30-37, and the two help interpret each other. The child in vv. 36-37 was linked with the "little ones" in v. 42. Much-needed teaching for the disciples (v. 31) continues. Jesus speaks, who after Peter's reference to him as Messiah (8:29) has twice talked of the impending death of the Son of Man and of resurrection/vindication by God. The Christology of Mark will provide links in the passage through use of the phrase "in my [Christ's] name," vv. 37, 38, 39, 41 (cf. "these little ones who believe [in me]," v. 42). But "discipleship talk" is the real theme.

The pericope begins with an incident about an "unauthorized" exorcist (v. 38). Its punch lines (vv. 39, 40, 41) move on into teachings, expressed almost poetically, about stumbling blocks and judgment (vv. 42-48) and, enigmatically, about salt (vv. 49-50). There are so many small units here that the preacher ought to consider concentrating on some one (or two) of them, without trying to cover all eleven verses; there is nothing sacrosanct about lectionary parameters, and no automatic unity conferred on the whole. If one seeks an underlying unity, it may lie in the fact that much of vv. 42-50 is addressed to the community of disciples who here represent the church community after Easter (hence the use of "Christ" in a proper sense). True, vv. 42-48 refer to the individual ("your hand, your foot" = you, singular; in 42, "any of you" is literally "whoever," changed for inclusive language reasons). But "these little ones who believe" (v. 42) assumes a community, as do "we/us" = "our group" in vv. 38, 40 and "you" (plural) in vv. 41 and 50b, as well as the references to you who "bear the name of Christ" in v. 41.

The opening discussion of the disciples with Jesus (vv. 38-40, form-critically a *Schulgespräch*) has John as spokesman, the only place in Mark he acts alone (cf. 1:19-20; 5:37; 9:2). This bunch of twelve, who still haven't gotten right who Jesus is (vv. 31-33) or what discipleship means (vv. 33-37), here is troubled about someone who has been effecting exorcisms in Jesus' name but who "does not follow us." So they tried to stop him. (For exorcisms by Jesus and his disciples, cf. 1:25-27, 34, 39; 7:26; 3:14-15; for Jewish exorcists, Matt. 12:27 = Luke 11:19 and Acts 19:13-17).

Use of the phrase "in your [Jesus'] name" is odd at this point, for Jesus never invokes his own name in a healing in Mark; that is a sign of post-Easter usage (Acts 3:6; 4:7, 10; 16:18; James 5:14). Odd also is the reference to "not following us" (v. 38), meaning the disciples and Jesus, in other words, the church and its leadership. Jesus forbids stopping this outsider, with the observation that to do a miracle "in my name" implies the person will not readily bad-mouth Jesus (v. 39). The optimist principle in v. 40 (and in Luke 9:50) is a statement of great tolerance: Let the Jesus-movement be open. Its obverse in Luke 11:23 = Matt. 12:30 (Q), "Whoever is not with me is against me," was spoken in a different context, not of people outside "our group" using Jesus' name, but of the charge that Jesus cast out demons in the name of Beelzebub (Satan). Practical theology is knowing when to apply which verse!

Verse 41 is an "amen" saying ("Truly I tell you"), extending the point of v. 40 with an example. Here Christians ("bear the name of Christ" is a paraphrase for a tangled textual picture that involves Greek for "in [the] name [of me]" and "because you are Christ's") are on the receiving end of the welcome cup of cold water (a gesture of hospitality). It reflects a missionary scene (and is so used in Matt. 10:40-42) and even broader kindness by those who are not Christians (as in Matt. 25:35, 37, 42, 44), though no more daring than Prov. 25:21-22. To the closed-minded disciples led by John, Jesus speaks for openness. Lectionary use of Num. 11:26-29 reinforces the theme of Mark 9:38-41. Commentators today see no direct influence on Mark of this narrative about Eldad and Medad (e.g., V. Taylor, 407). Caesar made a similar point, as reported by Cicero, *Oratio pro Ligario* 32: "We often have heard you say that we consider all as adversaries who are not with us; you consider all who are not against us as your (friends)."

This corrective to the misdirected zeal of disciples (and the church) is then balanced by two points about the internal life of the community and self-discipline. In vivid language about drowning (which was considered a particularly terrible form of execution), disciples are warned against putting stumbling blocks in the way of believers. (The imagery and church setting are even more specific in Matt. 18:6 [cf. Matt. 18:10, 15-22], as is the inevitability of stumblings caused by the world.) Anything is included that tempts or can trip up those who are vulnerable (children, marginal believers, the downtrodden, wearisome people, the unattractive—E. Schweizer, *Mark* [Richmond: John Knox, 1970], 198).

The second part (vv. 43-48) counsels tearing away whatever in each of us corrupts and prevents entry into life (vv. 44, 45), in other words, into the kingdom (v. 47). The verb *skandalizein*, "cause to stumble," links these verses together and to v. 42 ("stumbling block"). "Hell" (NRSV; footnote, literally *Gehenna*) deserves comment in a way that neither bypasses God's judgment nor goes beyond even v. 48 (= Isa. 66:24) into postbiblical pictures of eternal punishment ("hellfire and brimstone"). Such words are warnings to the individual about the seriousness to God eternally of one's discipleship.

Reference to fire in v. 48 leads on to v. 49, which suggests judgment, though some think of sacrifice and purification. Proverbial words about salt in v. 50a, coupled with 50b, suggest the need for disciples to preserve "salt" in and among themselves—perhaps by sharing salt at table (cf. Acts 1:4 Greek) in fellowship and peace, or in speech (Col. 4:6), or perhaps in readiness to be salted themselves for sacrifice (NRSV note, cf. Lev. 2:13; some commentators, assuming persecution of the church). Contrast the disciples' discussion about rank in 9:33-34.

Interpretation of such multi-allusive terms as "salt" and "stumbling" call out for ever new applications by the preacher, in what Mark sees as an open church, but gathered around Jesus Christ—self-disciplined, sacrifical of self, and serving the "little ones." Let there be no more insipid existence (Matt. 5:13 = Luke 14:34-35). All aboard for radical discipleship!